RETIREMENT ISSUES, PLANS AND LIFESTYLES

RETIREMENT SAVINGS AND CONFLICTED INVESTMENT ADVICE

COST AND PROTECTION ISSUES

FLORENCE P. MARSH
EDITOR

nova publishers
New York

Library of Congress Cataloging-in-Publication Data

ISBN: 978-1-63482-724-9

Published by Nova Science Publishers, Inc. † New York

CONTENTS

Preface		**vii**
Chapter 1	Traditional and Roth Individual Retirement Accounts (IRAs): A Primer *John J. Topoleski*	**1**
Chapter 2	The Effects of Conflicted Investment Advice on Retirement Savings *Council of Economic Advisers*	**21**
Chapter 3	401(K) Plans: Improved Regulation Could Better Protect Participants from Conflicts of Interest *United States Government Accountability Office*	**55**
Index		**123**

PREFACE

This book describes the primary features of two common retirement savings accounts that are available to individuals. It also examines the evidence on the cost of conflicted investment advice and its effects on Americans' retirement savings; and describes circumstances where service providers may have conflicts of interest in providing assistance related to the selection of investment options for plan sponsors and plan participants, and steps the Department of Labor (Labor) has taken to address conflicts of interest related to the selection of investment options.

Chapter 1 - In response to concerns over the adequacy of retirement savings, Congress has created incentives to encourage individuals to save more for retirement through a variety of retirement plans. Some retirement plans are employer-sponsored, such as 401(k) plans, and others are established by individual employees, such as Individual Retirement Accounts (IRAs).

This report describes the primary features of two common retirement savings accounts that are available to individuals. Although the accounts have many features in common, they differ in some very important aspects. Both traditional and Roth IRAs offer tax incentives to encourage individuals to save for retirement. Contributions to traditional IRAs may be tax-deductible for taxpayers who (1) are not covered by a retirement plan at their place of employment or (2) have income below specified limits. Contributions to Roth IRAs are not tax-deductible and eligibility is limited to those with incomes under specified limits.

The tax treatment of distributions from traditional and Roth IRAs differs. Distributions from traditional IRAs are generally included in taxable income whereas distributions from Roth IRAs are not included in taxable income. Some distributions may be subject to an additional 10% tax penalty, unless the distribution is for a reason specified in the Internal Revenue Code (for example, distributions from IRAs after the individual is aged 59 1/2 or older are not subject to the early withdrawal penalty).

Individuals may rollover eligible distributions from other retirement accounts (such as an account balance from a 401(k) plan upon leaving an employer) into IRAs. Rollovers preserve retirement savings by allowing investment earnings on the funds in the retirement accounts to accrue on a tax-deferred, in the case of traditional IRAs, or a tax-free basis, in the case of Roth IRAs.

The Retirement Savings Contribution Credit (also known as the Saver's Credit) is a nonrefundable tax credit of up to $1,000. It was authorized in 2001 to encourage retirement savings among individuals with income under specified limits.

This report explains the eligibility requirements, contribution limits, tax deductibility of contributions, and rules for withdrawing funds from the accounts. It also describes the Saver's Credit and provisions enacted after the Gulf of Mexico hurricanes in 2005 and the Midwestern storms in 2008 to exempt distributions to those affected by the disasters from the 10% early withdrawal penalty.

Chapter 2 - Americans' retirement income is derived from many sources, including Social Security, traditional pensions, employer-based retirement savings plans such as 401(k)s, and Individual Retirement Accounts (IRAs). While this landscape is familiar today, it reflects a dramatic change from the landscape 40 years ago. The share of working Americans covered by traditional pension plans—which offer a guaranteed income stream in retirement—has fallen sharply. Today, most workers participating in a retirement plan at work are covered by a defined contribution plan, such as a 401(k). Importantly, the income available in retirement from a defined contribution plan depends on both the amount initially saved and the return on those savings. The shift from traditional pensions to defined contribution plans raises important policy issues about investment responsibilities and the roles of individual households, employers, and investment advisers in ensuring the retirement security of Americans.

Defined contribution plans and IRAs are intricately linked, as the overwhelming majority of money flowing into IRAs comes from rollovers from an employer-based retirement plan, not direct IRA contributions. Collectively, more than 40 million American families have savings of more than $7 trillion in IRAs. More than 75 million families have an employer-based retirement plan, own an IRA, or both. Rollovers to IRAs exceeded $300 billion in 2012 and are expected to increase steadily in the coming years. The decision whether to roll over one's assets into an IRA can be confusing and the set of financial products that can be held in an IRA is vast, including savings accounts, money market accounts, mutual funds, exchange-traded funds, individual stocks and bonds, and annuities. Selecting and managing IRA investments can be a challenging and time-consuming task, frequently one of the most complex financial decisions in a person's life, and many Americans turn to professional advisers for assistance. However, financial advisers are often compensated through fees and commissions that depend on their clients' actions. Such fee structures generate acute conflicts of interest: the best recommendation for the saver may not be the best recommendation for the adviser's bottom line.

Chapter 3 - Recent volatility in financial markets highlights the need for prudent investment decisions if 401(k) plans are to provide an adequate source of retirement income. While plan sponsors and participants may receive help in assessing their investment choices, concerns have been raised about the impartiality of the advice provided. GAO was asked to describe circumstances where service providers may have conflicts of interest in providing assistance related to the selection of investment options for (1) plan sponsors and (2) plan participants, and (3) steps the Department of Labor (Labor) has taken to address conflicts of interest related to the selection of investment options.

In: Retirement Savings ...
Editor: Florence P. Marsh

ISBN: 978-1-63482-724-9

Chapter 1

TRADITIONAL AND ROTH INDIVIDUAL RETIREMENT ACCOUNTS (IRAS): A PRIMER*

John J. Topoleski

SUMMARY

In response to concerns over the adequacy of retirement savings, Congress has created incentives to encourage individuals to save more for retirement through a variety of retirement plans. Some retirement plans are employer-sponsored, such as 401(k) plans, and others are established by individual employees, such as Individual Retirement Accounts (IRAs).

This report describes the primary features of two common retirement savings accounts that are available to individuals. Although the accounts have many features in common, they differ in some very important aspects. Both traditional and Roth IRAs offer tax incentives to encourage individuals to save for retirement. Contributions to traditional IRAs may be tax-deductible for taxpayers who (1) are not covered by a retirement plan at their place of employment or (2) have income below specified limits. Contributions to Roth IRAs are not tax-deductible and eligibility is limited to those with incomes under specified limits.

* This is an edited, reformatted and augmented version of a Congressional Research Service publication RL34397, prepared for Members and Committees of Congress dated February 12, 2015.

The tax treatment of distributions from traditional and Roth IRAs differs. Distributions from traditional IRAs are generally included in taxable income whereas distributions from Roth IRAs are not included in taxable income. Some distributions may be subject to an additional 10% tax penalty, unless the distribution is for a reason specified in the Internal Revenue Code (for example, distributions from IRAs after the individual is aged 59 1/2 or older are not subject to the early withdrawal penalty).

Individuals may rollover eligible distributions from other retirement accounts (such as an account balance from a 401(k) plan upon leaving an employer) into IRAs. Rollovers preserve retirement savings by allowing investment earnings on the funds in the retirement accounts to accrue on a tax-deferred, in the case of traditional IRAs, or a tax-free basis, in the case of Roth IRAs.

The Retirement Savings Contribution Credit (also known as the Saver's Credit) is a nonrefundable tax credit of up to $1,000. It was authorized in 2001 to encourage retirement savings among individuals with income under specified limits.

This report explains the eligibility requirements, contribution limits, tax deductibility of contributions, and rules for withdrawing funds from the accounts. It also describes the Saver's Credit and provisions enacted after the Gulf of Mexico hurricanes in 2005 and the Midwestern storms in 2008 to exempt distributions to those affected by the disasters from the 10% early withdrawal penalty.

INTRODUCTION

Individual Retirement Accounts (IRAs) are tax-advantaged accounts that individuals (or married couples) can establish to accumulate funds for retirement. Depending on the type of IRA, contributions may be made on a pre-tax or post-tax basis, and investment earnings are either tax-deferred or tax-free.[1]

IRAs were first authorized by the Employee Retirement Income Security Act of 1974 (ERISA; P.L. 93-406). Originally limited to workers without pension coverage, all workers and spouses were made eligible for IRAs by the Economic Recovery Act of 1981 (P.L. 97-34). The Tax Reform Act of 1986 (P.L. 99-514) limited the eligibility for tax-deductible contributions to individuals whose employers do not sponsor plans and to those whose employers sponsor plans but who have earnings below certain thresholds. The Taxpayer Relief Act of 1997 (P.L. 105-34) allowed for certain penalty-free withdrawals and authorized the Roth IRA, which provides tax-free growth from after-tax contributions.

The Economic Growth and Tax Relief Reconciliation Act of 2001 (P.L. 107-16) significantly affected the contribution limits in these plans in three ways: (1) it increased the limits, (2) it indexed the limits to inflation, and (3) it allowed for individuals aged 50 and older to make additional "catch-up" contributions. Among other provisions, the Pension Protection Act of 2006 (P.L. 109-280) temporarily allowed for tax-free distributions for charitable contributions; made permanent the indexing of contribution limits to inflation; and allowed taxpayers to direct the Internal Revenue Service (IRS) to deposit tax refunds directly into an IRA.[2]

This report describes the two kinds of IRAs that individual employees can establish: traditional IRAs and Roth IRAs.[3] It describes the rules regarding eligibility, contributions, and withdrawals. It also describes a tax credit for retirement savings contributions. An *Appendix* explains rules related to penalty-free distributions for those affected by the 2005 Gulf of Mexico hurricanes and the 2008 Midwestern floods. The appendix also describes relief provided by the IRS to those affected by Hurricane Sandy in 2012.

IRA ASSETS AND SOURCES OF FUNDS

Table 1 contains data on the end-of-year assets in traditional and Roth IRAs from 2004 to 2013. According to the Investment Company Institute, traditional IRAs held much more in assets than Roth IRAs. At the end of 2013, there was $6.0 trillion held in traditional IRAs and $505 billion held in Roth IRAs. Within traditional IRAs, more funds flowed from rollovers from employer-sponsored pensions compared with funds from regular contributions.[4]

Table 1. Traditional and Roth IRAs: End of Year Assets (in billions of dollars)

	2004	2005	2006	2007	2008	2009	2010	2011	2012	2013
Traditio-nal IRAs	$2,957	$3,034	$3,722	$4,187	$3,257	$3,941	$4,340	$4,531	$5,109	$6,019
Roth IRAs	140	156	196	232	177	239	355	365	420	505

Source: The Congressional Research Service (CRS) table using data from the Investment Company Institute, The U.S. Retirement Market, Third Quarter 2014, Table 8, available at http://www.ici.org/info/ ret_14_q3_data.xls.

For example, in 2010 (the latest year for which such data are available) funds from rollovers were $288.4 billion, whereas funds from contributions were only $12.8 billion.[5]

TRADITIONAL IRAS

Traditional IRAs are funded by workers' contributions, which may be tax-deductible. The contributions accrue investment earnings in an account, and these earnings are used as a basis for retirement income. Among the benefits of traditional IRAs, two are (1) pre-tax contributions provide larger bases for accumulating investment earnings and, thus, provide larger account balances at retirement than if the money had been placed in taxable accounts; and (2) taxes are paid when funds are distributed. Since income tax rates in retirement are often lower than during working life, traditional IRA holders are likely to pay less in taxes when contributions are withdrawn than when the income was earned.

Eligibility

Individuals under 701/2 years old in a year and receive taxable compensation can set up and contribute to IRAs. Examples of compensation include wages, salaries, tips, commissions, self-employment income, alimony, and nontaxable combat pay. Individuals who receive income only from non-compensation sources cannot contribute to IRAs.

Contributions

Individuals may contribute either their gross compensation or the contribution limit, whichever is lower. In 2015, the contribution limit is $5,500 unchanged from 2014. Since 2009, the contribution limit has been indexed to inflation, although the change in the Consumer Price Index was insufficient for a cost-of-living adjustment to the 2011 or 2012 contribution limit. Individuals aged 50 and older may make additional $1,000 catch-up contributions. For households that file a joint return, spouses may contribute an amount equal to the couple's total compensation (reduced by the spouse's IRA contributions) or the contribution limit ($5,500 each, if younger than the age of 50, and

$6,500 each, if 50 years or older), whichever is lower. Contributions that exceed the contribution limit and are not withdrawn by the due date for the tax return for that year are considered excess contributions and are subject to a 6% "excess contribution" tax. Contributions made between January 1 and April 15 may be designated for either the current year or the previous year.

Because IRAs were intended for workers without an employer-sponsored pension to save for retirement, contributions to an IRA may only come from work income, such as wages and tips. The following non-compensation sources of income cannot be used for IRA contributions:

- earnings from property, interest, or dividends;
- pension or annuity income;
- deferred compensation;
- income from partnerships for which an individual does not provide services that are a material income-producing factor; and
- foreign earned income.

Investment Options

IRAs can be set up through many financial institutions, such as banks, credit unions, mutual funds, life insurance companies, or stock brokerages. Individuals have an array of investment choices offered by the financial institutions and can transfer their accounts to other financial institutions at will.

Several transactions could result in additional taxes or the loss of IRA status. These transactions include borrowing from IRAs; using IRAs as collateral for loans; selling property to IRAs; and investing in collectibles like artwork, antiques, metals, gems, stamps, alcoholic beverages, and most coins.[6]

Deductibility of Contributions

IRA contributions may be non-tax-deductible, partially tax-deductible, or fully tax-deductible, depending on whether the individual or spouse is covered by a pension plan at work and the level of adjusted gross income (AGI). Individuals are covered by a retirement plan if (1) the individuals or their employers have made contributions to a defined contribution pension plan or

(2) the individuals are eligible for a defined benefit pension plan (even if they refuse participation).

For individuals and households not covered by a pension plan at work, *Table 2* contains the income levels at which they may deduct all, some, or none of their IRA contributions, depending on the spouse's pension coverage and the household's AGI. Individuals without employer-sponsored pensions and, if married, whose spouse also does not have pension coverage may deduct up to the contribution limit from their income taxes regardless of their AGI.

For individuals and households who are covered by a pension plan at work, *Table 3* contains the income levels at which they may deduct all, some, or none of their IRA contributions, depending on the individual's or household's AGI.

Table 2. Deductibility of IRA Contributions for Individuals

Filing Status	2014 Adjusted Gross Income	2015 Adjusted Gross Income	Deduction Allowed
Single, head of household, qualifying widow(er), or married filing jointly or separately with a spouse who is not covered by a plan at work	Any amount	Any amount	Full deduction
Married filing jointly or separately with a spouse who is covered by a plan at work	$181,000 or less	$183,000 or less	full deduction
	More than $181,000 but less than$191,000	More than $183,000 deduction but less than$193,000	Partial
	$191,000 or more	$193,000 or more	No deduction
Married filing separately with a spouse who is covered by a plan at work	Less than $10,000	Less than $10,000	Partial deduction
	$10,000 or more	$10,000 or more	No deduction

Source: IRS Publication 590, available at http://www.irs.gov/publications/p590/ and IRS News Release IR-2014-99 available at http://www.irs.gov/uac/Newsroom/IRS-Announces-2015-Pension-Plan-Limitations-1.

Individuals may still contribute to IRAs up to the contribution limit even if the contribution is non-deductible. Non-deductible contributions come from post-tax income, not pre-tax income. One advantage to placing post-tax income in traditional IRAs is that investment earnings on nondeductible contributions are not taxed until distributed. Only contributions greater than the contribution limits as described above are considered excess contributions. Worksheets for computing partial deductions are included in "IRS Publication 590, Individual Retirement Arrangements (IRAs)."[7]

Table 3. Deductibility of IRA Contributions for Individuals Covered by a Plan at Work for 2014 and 2015

Filing Status	2014 Adjusted Gross Income	2015 Adjusted Gross Income	Deduction Allowed
Single or head of household	$60,000 or less	$61,000 or less	Full deduction
	More than $60,000 but less than $70,000	More than $61,000 but less than $71,000	Partial deduction
	$69,000 or more	$71,000 or more	No deduction
Married filing jointly or qualifying widow(er)	$96,000 or less	$98,000 or less	Full deduction
	More than $96,000 but less than $116,000	More than $98,000 but less than $118,000	Partial deduction
	$116,000 or more	$118,000 or more	No deduction
Married filing separately	Less than $10,000	Less than $10,000	Partial deduction
	$10,000 or more	$10,000 or more	No deduction

Source: IRS Publication 590, available at http://www.irs.gov/publications/p590/ and IRS News Release IR-2014-99 available at http://www.irs.gov/uac/Newsroom/IRS-Announces-2015-Pension-Plan-Limitations-1.

Withdrawals

Withdrawals from IRAs are subject to income tax in the year that they are received.[8] Early distributions are withdrawals made before the age of 591,4. Early distributions may be subject to an additional 10% penalty.

To ensure that IRAs are used for retirement income and not for bequests, IRA holders must begin making withdrawals by April 1 of the year after reaching the age of 701,4 (i.e., the required beginning date). The minimum amount that must be withdrawn (i.e., the required minimum distribution) is calculated by dividing the account balance on December 31 of the year preceding the distribution by the IRA owner's life expectancy as found in IRS

Publication 590.[9] Although females live longer on average than males, the IRS does not separate life expectancy tables for males and females for this purpose.[10] Required minimum distributions must be received by December 31 of each year. Failure to take the required minimum distribution results in a 50% excise tax on the amount not distributed as required. Congress suspended the Required Minimum Distribution (RMD) provision for 2009.[11]

Beginning in 2007, distributions from IRAs after the age of 701,4 could be made directly to qualified charities and excluded from gross income. This provision for Qualified Charitable Distributions expired December 31, 2013.[12]

Early Distributions

Early distributions are withdrawals made before the age of 591,4. Early distributions—just like distributions after the age of 591,4—are subject to federal income tax. To discourage the use of IRA funds for pre-retirement uses, most early distributions are subject to a 10% tax penalty.[13] The early withdrawal penalty does not apply to distributions before the age of 591,4 if they

- occur if the individual is a beneficiary of a deceased IRA owner;
- occur if the individual is disabled;
- are in substantially equal payments over the account holder's life expectancy;
- are received after separation from employment after the age of 55;
- are for unreimbursed medical expenses in excess of 7.5% of AGI;
- are for medical insurance premiums in the case of unemployment;
- are used for higher education expenses;
- are used to build, buy, or rebuild a first home up to a $10,000 withdrawal limit;
- occur if the individual is a reservist called to active duty after September 11, 2001;
- were distributions to residents in areas affected by Hurricanes Katrina, Rita, and Wilma from around the storms' landfalls to January 1, 2007; or
- were distributions to residents in areas affected by the Midwestern floods in 2008 from after the applicable disaster date and before January 1, 2010.

While individuals may make early withdrawals from IRAs without a reason, they will be subject to the 10% tax penalty unless they meet one of the conditions above. There are no other general "hardship" exceptions for penalty-free distributions from IRAs.

Rollovers

Rollovers are transfers of assets from one retirement plan to another upon separation from the original employer. Rollovers are not subject to the 591,4 rule, the 10% penalty, or the contribution limit. Rollovers can come from traditional IRAs, employers' qualified retirement plans (e.g., 401(k) plans), deferred compensation plans of state or local governments (Section 457 plans), tax-sheltered annuities (Section 403(b) plans), or the Thrift Savings Plan for federal employees.

Rollovers can be either direct trustee-to-trustee transfers[14] or issued directly to individuals who then deposit the rollovers into traditional IRAs. Individuals have 60 days to make rollover contributions. Rollovers not completed within 60 days are considered taxable distributions and may be subject to the 10% early withdrawal penalty. In addition, in cases where individuals directly receive a rollover, 20% of the rollover is withheld for tax purposes. Direct trustee-totrustee transfers are not subject to withholding taxes. In cases where individuals directly receive a rollover, they must have an amount equal to the 20% withheld available from other sources to place in the new IRA. If the entire distribution is rolled over within 60 days, the amount withheld is applied to individuals' income taxes paid for the year.

Rollovers Limited to One Per Year

A January 2014 U.S. Tax Court decision requires that, in certain circumstances, individuals are limited to a total of one rollover per year for their IRAs.[15] Rollovers subject to this rule are those between two IRAs in which an individual receives funds from an IRA and deposits the funds into a different IRA within 60 days. The one-rollover-per-year limit applies to rollovers between two traditional IRAs or two Roth IRAs. It does not apply to rollovers from a traditional IRA to a Roth IRA. The limitation does not apply to trustee-to-trustee transfers or rollovers from qualified pension plans (such as from 401(k) plans).

Inherited IRAs

When the owner of an IRA dies, ownership passes to the account's designated beneficiary or, if no beneficiary has been named, to the decedent's estate. Federal law has different distribution requirements depending on whether the new owner is a

- designated beneficiary who is the former owner's spouse;
- designated beneficiary who is not the former owner's spouse; or
- non-designated beneficiary.

The distribution rules are summarized in *Table 4*. The distribution rules also depend on whether the IRA owner died prior to the required beginning date, the date on which distributions from the account must begin. It is April 1 of the year following the year in which the owner of an IRA reaches the age of 701/2. Distributions from inherited IRAs are taxable income but are not subject to the 10% early withdrawal penalty. Failure to take the RMD results in a 50% excise tax on the amount not distributed as required.

Designated spouse beneficiaries who treat inherited IRAs as their own can roll over inherited IRAs into traditional IRAs or, to the extent that the inherited IRAs are taxable, into qualified employer plans (such as 401(k), 403(b), or 457 plans). Non-spouse beneficiaries cannot roll over any amount into or out of inherited IRAs. In some cases, IRAs have beneficiaries' distributions requirements that are more stringent than those summarized in *Table 4*. For example, an IRA's plan documents could require that a designated spouse or designated nonspouse beneficiary distribute all assets in the IRA by the end of the fifth year of the year following the IRA owner's death. In such a case, the beneficiary would not have the option to take distributions over a longer period of time. Unless the IRA plan documents specify otherwise, it is possible to take distributions faster than required in *Table 4*. For example, a beneficiary may elect to distribute all assets in a single year. In such a case, the entire amount distributed is taxable income for that year.

Table 4. Inherited IRA Distribution Rules

	Owner Dies Before Required Beginning Date	Owner Dies after Required Beginning Date
Spouse is named as the designated beneficiary	Treat as own, does not have to take any distribution until	Treat as own, does not have to take any distribution until

	Owner Dies Before Required Beginning Date	Owner Dies after Required Beginning Date
	the age of 70½, but is subject to the 59½ rule, or	the age of 70½, but is subject to the 59½ rule, or
	Keep in decedent's name and take distributions based on own life expectancy. Distributions do not have to begin until decedent would have turned 70½.	Keep in decedent's name and take distributions based on own life expectancy.
A nonspouse is named as the designated beneficiary	Take distributions based on life expectancy for beneficiary's age as of birthday in the year following the year of the owner's death, reduced by one for each year since owner's death. If the nonspouse beneficiary does not take a distribution in year of owner's death, then all IRA assets must be distributed by the end of the fifth year of the year following the IRA owner's death.	Take distributions based on the longer of (1) beneficiary's life expectancy, or (2) owner's life expectancy using age as of birthday in the year of death, reduced by one for year after the year of death.
Beneficiary is not named	Must distribute all IRA assets by the end of the fifth year of the year following the IRA owner's death.	Take a yearly distribution based on the owner's age as of birthday in the year of death, reduced by one for each year after the year of death.

Source: IRS Publication 590, available at http://www.irs.gov/publications/p590/.

Notes: The required beginning date is the date on which distributions from the account must begin. It is April 1 of the year following the year in which the owner of an IRA reaches the age of 701/4.

ROTH IRAS

Roth IRAs were authorized by the Taxpayer Relief Act of 1997 (P.L. 105-34). The key differences between traditional and Roth IRAs are that contributions to Roth IRAs are made with after-tax funds and qualified distributions are not included in taxable income; hence, investment earnings accrue free of taxes.[16]

Eligibility and Contribution Limits

In contrast to traditional IRAs, Roth IRAs have income limits for eligibility. *Table 5* lists the adjusted gross incomes at which individuals may make the maximum contribution and the ranges in which this contribution limit is reduced. For example, a 40-year-old single taxpayer with income of $90,000 can contribute $5,500 in 2015. A similar taxpayer making $120,000 would be subject to a reduced contribution limit, whereas a taxpayer with income of $140,000 would be ineligible to contribute to a Roth IRA.

Table 5. Roth IRA Eligibility and Contribution Limits for 2014 and 2015

Filing Status	2014 Modified Adjusted Gross Income (AGI)	2014 Contribution Limits	2015 Modified Adjusted Gross Income (AGI)	2015 Contribution Limits
Single, head of household, married filing separately (and did not live with spouse at any time during the year)	Less than $114,000 At least $114,000 but less than $129,000 $129,000 or more	$5,500 ($6,500 if 50 years or older) or AGI, whichever is smaller Reduced contribution limit Ineligible to contribute	Less than $116,000 At least $116,000 but less than $131,000 $131,000 or more	$5,500 ($6,500 if 50 years or older) or AGI, whichever is smaller Reduced contribution limit Ineligible to contribute
Married filing separately and lived with spouse at any time during the year	Less than $10,000 $10,000 or more	Reduced contribution limit Ineligible to contribute	Less than $10,000 $10,000 or more	Reduced contribution limit Ineligible to contribute
Married filing jointly, qualifying widow(er)	Less than $181,000	$5,500 each ($6,500 each if 50 and older) or AGI, whichever is smaller	Less than $183,000	$5,500 each ($6,500 each if 50 and older) or AGI, whichever is smaller

Filing Status	2014 Modified Adjusted Gross Income (AGI)	2014 Contribution Limits	2015 Modified Adjusted Gross Income (AGI)	2015 Contribution Limits
	At least $181,000 but less than $191,000	Reduced contribution limit	At least $183,000 but less than $193,000	Reduced contribution limit
	$191,000 or more	Ineligible to contribute	$193,000 or more	Ineligible to contribute

Source: IRS Publication 590, available at http://www.irs.gov/publications/p590/ and IRS News Release IR-2014-99 available at http://www.irs.gov/uac/Newsroom/IRS-Announces-2015-Pension-Plan-Limitations-1.

Individuals aged 50 and older can make additional $1,000 catch-up contributions. The AGI limit for eligibility has been adjusted for inflation since 2007; beginning in 2009, the traditional and Roth IRA contribution limit has also been adjusted for inflation. A worksheet for computing reduced Roth IRA contribution limits is provided in IRS Publication 590.

Investment Options

Roth IRAs must be designated as such when they are set up. As with traditional IRAs, they can be set up through many financial institutions. Transactions prohibited within traditional IRAs are also prohibited within Roth IRAs.

Conversions and Rollovers

Individuals may convert amounts from traditional IRAs, SEP-IRAs, or SIMPLE-IRAs to Roth IRAs.[17] Since 2008, individuals have been able to rollover distributions directly from qualified retirement plans to Roth IRAs. Amounts that would have been included in income if the conversion had not been made must be included in income. Conversions can be a trustee-totrustee transfer, a same trustee transfer by redesignating the IRA as a Roth IRA, or a rollover directly to the account holder. Inherited IRAs cannot be converted.

The rules for rollovers that apply to traditional IRAs, including completing a rollover within 60 days, also apply. Additionally, withdrawals from a converted IRA prior to five years from the beginning of the year of conversion are non-qualified distributions and are subject to a 10% penalty.

Tax-free withdrawals from one Roth IRA transferred to another Roth IRA are allowed if completed within 60 days. Rollovers from Roth IRAs to other types of IRAs or to employer-sponsored retirement plans are not allowed.

Withdrawals

The three kinds of distributions from Roth IRAs are (1) return of regular contributions, (2) qualified distributions, and (3) non-qualified distributions. Returns of regular contributions and qualified distributions are not included as part of taxable income.

Return of Regular Contributions

Distributions from Roth IRAs that are a return of regular contributions are not included in gross income nor are they subject to the 10% penalty on early distributions.

Qualified Distributions

Qualified distributions must satisfy both of the following:

- they are made after the five-year period beginning with the first taxable year for which a Roth IRA contribution was made,[18] and
- they are made on or after the age of 591/2; because of disability; to a beneficiary or estate after death; or to purchase, build, or rebuild a first home up to a $10,000 lifetime limit.

Non-Qualified Distributions

Distributions that are neither returns of regular contributions nor qualified distributions are considered non-qualified distributions. Although individuals might have several Roth IRAs from which withdrawals can be made, for tax purposes non-qualified distributions are assumed to be made in the following order:

1. the return of regular contributions,
2. conversion contributions on a first-in-first-out basis, and
3. earnings on contributions.

Non-qualified distributions may have to be included as part of income for tax purposes. A worksheet is available in IRS Publication 590 to determine the taxable portion of non-qualified distributions. A 10% penalty applies to non-qualified distributions unless one of the exceptions in 26 U.S.C. Section 72(t) applies. The exceptions are identical to those previously listed for early withdrawals from traditional IRAs.

Distributions after Roth IRA Owner's Death

If the owner of a Roth IRA dies, the distribution rules depend on whether the beneficiary is the spouse or a nonspouse. If the beneficiary is the spouse, then the spouse becomes the new owner of the inherited Roth IRA. If the spouse chooses not to treat the inherited Roth IRA as their own, or if the beneficiary is a nonspouse, then there are two options. The beneficiary can distribute the entire interest in the Roth IRA (1) by the end of the fifth calendar year after the year of the owner's death, or (2) over the beneficiary's life expectancy. As with an inherited traditional IRA, a spouse can delay distributions until the decedent would have reached the age of 701/2.

Distributions from inherited Roth IRAs are generally free of income tax. The beneficiary may be subject to taxes if the owner of a Roth IRA dies before the end of (1) the five-year period beginning with the first taxable year for which a contribution was made to a Roth IRA or (2) the five-year period starting with the year of a conversion from a traditional IRA to a Roth IRA. The distributions are treated as described in the "Non-Qualified Distributions" section, above.

RETIREMENT SAVINGS CONTRIBUTION CREDIT

Thc Economic Growth and Tax Relief Reconciliation Act of 2001 (P.L. 107-16) authorized a nonrefundable tax credit of up to $1,000 for eligible individuals, or $2,000 if filing a joint return, who contribute to IRAs or employer-sponsored retirement plans.[19] The tax credit is in addition to the tax deduction for contributions to traditional IRAs or other employer-sponsored pension plans. To receive the credit, taxpayers must be at least 18 years old, not full-time students, not an exemption on someone else's tax return, and have AGI less than certain limits. The limits are in *Table 6*. For example, individuals who make a $2,000 IRA contribution in 2014, have income of

$15,000, and list their filing status as single would be able to reduce their 2014 tax liability by up to $1,000. Taxpayers must file form 1040, 1040A, or 1040NR. It is not available on form 1040EZ, which may limit the use of the credit.

Table 6. Retirement Saving Contribution Credit Income Limits for 2014 and 2015

Filing Status	2014 Income Limits	2015 Income Limits	Percentage Credit
Single, Married Filing Separately,	$1 to $18,000	$1 to $18,250	50%
Qualifying Widow(er)	$18,001 to $19,500	$18,251 to $19,750	20%
	$19,501 to $30,000	$19,751 to $30,500	10%
	more than $30,000	more than $30,500	0%
Head of Household	$1 to $27,000	$1 to $27,375	50%
	$27,001 to $29,250	$27,376 to $29,625	20%
	$29,251 to $45,000	$29,626 to $45,750	10%
	more than $45,000	more than $45,750	0%
Married Filing Jointly	$1 to $36,000	$1 to $36,500	50%
	$36,001 to $39,000	$36,501 to $39,500	20%
	$39,001 to $60,000	$39,501 to $61,000	10%
	more than $60,000	more than $61,000	0%

Source: IRS Publication 590, available at http://www.irs.gov/publications/p590/ and IRS News Release IR-2014-99 available at http://www.irs.gov/uac/Newsroom/IRS-Announces-2015-Pension-Plan-Limitations-1.

APPENDIX. QUALIFIED DISTRIBUTIONS RELATED TO NATURAL DISASTERS

As part of the response to the 2005 hurricanes that affected the communities on and near the Gulf of Mexico, Congress approved provisions that exempted individuals affected by the storms from the 10% early withdrawal penalty for withdrawals from IRA. In 2008, Congress approved similar provisions in response to the storms and flooding in certain Midwestern states. Following Hurricane Sandy in October 2013, the Internal Revenue Service (IRS) eased certain requirements for hardship distributions from defined contribution plans. The IRS was unable to exempt distributions from retirement plans from the 10% early withdrawal penalty because such an exemption requires congressional authorization.

Qualified Distributions Related to Hurricanes Katrina, Rita, and Wilma

In response to Hurricanes Katrina, Rita, and Wilma, Congress approved the Gulf Opportunity Zone Act of 2005 (P.L. 109-135). The act amended the Internal Revenue Code to allow residents in areas affected by these storms who suffered economic losses to take penalty-free distributions up to $100,000 from their retirement plans, including traditional and Roth IRAs. The distributions must have been received after August 24, 2005 (Katrina), September 22, 2005 (Rita), or October 22, 2005 (Wilma), and before January 1, 2007. The distributions are taxable income and can be reported as income either in the year received or over three years (e.g., a $30,000 distribution made in May 2006, can be reported as $10,000 of income in 2006, 2007, and 2008). Alternatively, part or all of the distribution may be repaid to the retirement plan within three years of receiving the distribution without being considered taxable income.

Qualified Distributions Related to the Midwestern Disaster Relief Area

In response to severe storms, tornados, and flooding that occurred in certain Midwestern states, the Heartland Disaster Tax Relief Act of 2008 allows residents of specified Midwest areas to take penalty-free distributions up to $100,000 from their retirement plans, including traditional and Roth IRAs. This act was passed as Division C of P.L. 110-343, the Emergency Economic Stabilization Act of 2008. The bill amends 26 U.S.C. 1400Q, which was enacted as part of the Gulf Opportunity Zone Act of 2005 (P.L. 109-135). The distributions must be received after the date in which the President declared an area to be a major disaster area and before January 1, 2010.[20] Apart from the dates and the areas affected, the provisions are identical to the provisions for individuals who were affected by Hurricanes Katrina, Rita, and Wilma.

Hurricane Sandy Relief

No legislation was passed that would have (1) exempted individuals in areas affected by Hurricane Sandy from the 10% penalty for early withdrawals from IRAs or defined contribution retirement plans or (2) eased requirements for loans from defined contribution pensions for individuals affected by Hurricane Sandy in 2012.[21]

The IRS eased requirements for hardship distributions in areas affected by Hurricane Sandy. Among the relief offered by the IRS in Announcement 2012-44, "Plan administrators may rely upon representations from the employee or former employee as to the need for and amount of a hardship distribution" rather than require documentation from the employee of the need.[22] The relief offered by the IRS did not include an exemption from the 10% penalty for distributions before the age of 591/2. Exemptions from the 10% penalty require congressional authorization. In addition, in the announcement, the IRS suspended the provision that requires an individual to suspend contributions to a 401(K) and 403(b) plans for the six months following a hardship distribution.

End Notes

[1] For more information on the tax treatment of retirement savings, including IRAs, see U.S. Congress, Joint Committee on Taxation, Present Law And Background Relating To The Tax Treatment Of Retirement Savings, prepared by Joint Committee on Taxation, 112th Cong., 2nd sess., April 13, 2012, JCX-32-12.

[2] See also 26 U.S.C. §408 for traditional IRAs and 26 U.S.C. §408A for Roth IRAs.

[3] For additional information, see CRS Report RL30255, Individual Retirement Accounts (IRAs): Issues and Proposed Expansion, by Thomas L. Hungerford and Jane G. Gravelle, and CRS Report RS22019, IRAs and Other Savings Incentives: A Brief Overview, by Jane G. Gravelle. There are also two kinds of IRAs established by employers for employees in small businesses: Simplified Employee Pensions (SEP-IRA) and Savings Incentive Match Plans for Employees (SIMPLE-IRA).

[4] Generally, rollovers are tax-free distributions of assets from one retirement plan that are contributed to a second retirement plan. Regular contributions are contributions to IRAs that are made from individuals' pre- or post-tax income (subject to the rules of the particular type of IRA).

[5] See the Investment Company Institute, The U.S. Retirement Market, Third Quarter 2014, Table 9, available at http://www.ici.org/info/ret_14_q3_data.xls.

[6] Gold, silver, and platinum coins issued by the U.S. Treasury, and gold, silver, palladium, and platinum bullion are permissible.

[7] The publication is available on the IRS website at http://www.irs.gov/pub/irs-pdf/p590.pdf.

[8] For a detailed explanation of withdrawals from IRAs, see CRS Report R40192, Early Withdrawals and Required Minimum Distributions in Retirement Accounts: Issues for Congress, by John J. Topoleski.

[9] Life expectancy is calculated differently depending on whether the account holder (1) is single and an IRA beneficiary, (2) has a spouse who is more than 10 years younger, (3) has a

spouse who is not more than 10 years younger, (4) whose spouse is not the sole beneficiary, or (5) is unmarried.

[10] The Supreme Court ruled in Arizona Governing Comm. vs. Norris, 463 U.S. 1073 (1983), that employer-provided pension plans must use unisex tables in calculating monthly annuity benefits. Citing this ruling, the IRS constructs its own unisex life expectancy tables. See 26 U.S.C. §417(e)(3)(A)(ii).

[11] Although proposals were introduced to suspend the RMD in years after 2009, Congress did not enact any. See CRS Report R40192, Early Withdrawals and Required Minimum Distributions in Retirement Accounts: Issues for Congress, by John J. Topoleski.

[12] See CRS Report RS22766, Qualified Charitable Distributions from Individual Retirement Accounts: Features and Legislative History, by John J. Topoleski and Gary Sidor.

[13] See 26 U.S.C. §72(t).

[14] A trustee-to-trustee transfer is a transfer of funds made directly between two financial institutions. The individual does not take possession of the funds at any point.

[15] See Bobrow vs. Commissioner - U.S. Tax Court, available at http://www.ustaxcourt.gov/InOpHistoric/bobrowmemo.nega.TCM.WPD.pdf. Prior to this decision, the IRS applied the one-rollover-per-year on an IRA-by-IRA basis.

[16] Roth IRAs are named for former Senator William Roth (DE).

[17] Prior to January 1, 2010, only individuals with income under specified thresholds were eligible to make conversions from traditional to Roth IRAs. The Tax Increase Prevention and Reconciliation Act of 2005 (TIPRA; P.L. 109-222) eliminated the income thresholds.

[18] The five-year period is not necessarily five calendar years. Contributions made from January 1 to April 15 could be considered made in the previous tax year.

[19] See also CRS Report RS21795, The Retirement Savings Tax Credit: A Fact Sheet, by John J. Topoleski.

[20] The disaster areas are limited to Arkansas, Illinois, Indiana, Iowa, Kansas, Michigan, Minnesota, Missouri, Nebraska, and Wisconsin.

[21] H.R. 2137, the Hurricane Sandy Tax Relief Act of 2013, introduced by Representative Bill Pascrell on May 23, 2013, would have provided an exemption to the 10% early withdrawal penalty for retirement account distributions for those affected by Hurricane Sandy.

[22] See 26 CFR 1.401(k)-1.

In: Retirement Savings ...
Editor: Florence P. Marsh

ISBN: 978-1-63482-724-9

Chapter 2

THE EFFECTS OF CONFLICTED INVESTMENT ADVICE ON RETIREMENT SAVINGS*

Council of Economic Advisers

EXECUTIVE SUMMARY

Americans' retirement income is derived from many sources, including Social Security, traditional pensions, employer-based retirement savings plans such as 401(k)s, and Individual Retirement Accounts (IRAs). While this landscape is familiar today, it reflects a dramatic change from the landscape 40 years ago. The share of working Americans covered by traditional pension plans—which offer a guaranteed income stream in retirement—has fallen sharply. Today, most workers participating in a retirement plan at work are covered by a defined contribution plan, such as a 401(k). Importantly, the income available in retirement from a defined contribution plan depends on both the amount initially saved and the return on those savings. The shift from traditional pensions to defined contribution plans raises important policy issues about investment responsibilities and the roles of individual households, employers, and investment advisers in ensuring the retirement security of Americans.

Defined contribution plans and IRAs are intricately linked, as the overwhelming majority of money flowing into IRAs comes from rollovers from

---

* This is an edited, reformatted and augmented version of a report issued by the Executive Office of the White House, February 2015.

an employer-based retirement plan, not direct IRA contributions. Collectively, more than 40 million American families have savings of more than $7 trillion in IRAs. More than 75 million families have an employer-based retirement plan, own an IRA, or both. Rollovers to IRAs exceeded $300 billion in 2012 and are expected to increase steadily in the coming years. The decision whether to roll over one's assets into an IRA can be confusing and the set of financial products that can be held in an IRA is vast, including savings accounts, money market accounts, mutual funds, exchange-traded funds, individual stocks and bonds, and annuities. Selecting and managing IRA investments can be a challenging and time-consuming task, frequently one of the most complex financial decisions in a person's life, and many Americans turn to professional advisers for assistance. However, financial advisers are often compensated through fees and commissions that depend on their clients' actions. Such fee structures generate acute conflicts of interest: the best recommendation for the saver may not be the best recommendation for the adviser's bottom line.

This report examines the evidence on the cost of conflicted investment advice and its effects on Americans' retirement savings, focusing on IRAs. Investment losses due to conflicted advice result from the incentives conflicted payments generate for financial advisers to steer savers into products or investment strategies that provide larger payments to the adviser but are not necessarily the best choice for the saver.

The Council of Economic Advisers' survey of the literature finds that:

- Conflicted advice leads to lower investment returns. Savers receiving conflicted advice earn returns roughly 1 percentage point lower each year (for example, conflicted advice reduces what would be a 6 percent return to a 5 percent return).
- An estimated $1.7 trillion of IRA assets are invested in products that generally provide payments that generate conflicts of interest. Thus, we estimate the aggregate annual cost of conflicted advice is about $17 billion each year.
- A retiree who receives conflicted advice when rolling over a 401(k) balance to an IRA at retirement will lose an estimated 12 percent of the value of his or her savings if drawn down over 30 years. If a retiree receiving conflicted advice takes withdrawals at the rate possible absent conflicted advice, his or her savings would run out more than 5 years earlier.
- The average IRA rollover for individuals 55 to 64 in 2012 was more than $100,000; losing 12 percent from conflicted advice has the same

effect on feasible future withdrawals as if $12,000 was lost in the transfer.

The conclusions of this report are based on a careful review of the relevant academic literature but, as with any such analysis, are subject to uncertainty. However, this uncertainty should not mask the essential finding of this report: conflicted advice leads to large and economically meaningful costs for Americans' retirement savings. Even a far more conservative estimate of the investment losses due to conflicted advice, such as half of a percentage point, would indicate annual losses of more than $8 billion. On the other hand, if conflicted advice affects a larger portion of IRA assets than the $1.7 trillion considered here—or if the estimate were extended to other forms of retirement savings—the total annual cost would exceed $17 billion.

I. The U.S. Retirement System

Americans' retirement income comes from many sources. Social Security provides a basic foundation for retirement security. Traditional pensions, employer-based retirement savings plans such as 401(k)s, and Individual Retirement Accounts (IRAs) allow workers to set aside additional earnings explicitly designated for retirement in a tax-advantaged way. (Table 1 provides an overview of these forms of savings.) Other savings, whether in a bank account or a home, provide additional resources that can be tapped in retirement. While this landscape is familiar today, it reflects a dramatic change from the landscape 40 years ago. The share of working Americans covered by traditional pension plans—which offer a guaranteed income stream in retirement—has fallen sharply. Today the majority of workers participating in a retirement plan at work are covered by a defined contribution plan, such as a 401(k).

Figure 1 shows the composition of Americans' tax-preferred retirement savings for the period 1978 to 2013. In 1978, traditional pensions accounted for nearly 70 percent of all retirement assets. Defined contribution plans accounted for less than 20 percent and IRAs accounted for only 2 percent. Annuities accounted for the remainder.[2] By the end of 2013, traditional pensions accounted for only 35 percent of retirement assets, a decrease of 32 percentage points; defined contribution plans and IRAs accounted for more than half of all retirement assets.

Table 1. Select Forms of Tax-Preferred Retirement Savings [1]

Type of Plan	Description
Defined Benefit (DB) Plan	Traditional pensions that provide a guaranteed payment for life. Benefits typically determined according to a formula involving some combination of age, earnings, and tenure.
Defined Contribution (DC) Plan	Retirement savings plans that allow employee and/or employer contributions. Benefits depend on both the amount saved and the investment returns net of fees on those assets. Workers bear the risk associated with asset returns. Examples include 401(k)s, 403(b)s, the Federal Thrift Savings Plan, and profit-sharing plans.
Individual Retirement Account (IRA)	Retirement savings plans independent of employment that allow individual contributions. Benefits depend on both the amount saved and the investment returns net of fees on those assets. Individual savers bear the risk associated with asset returns.

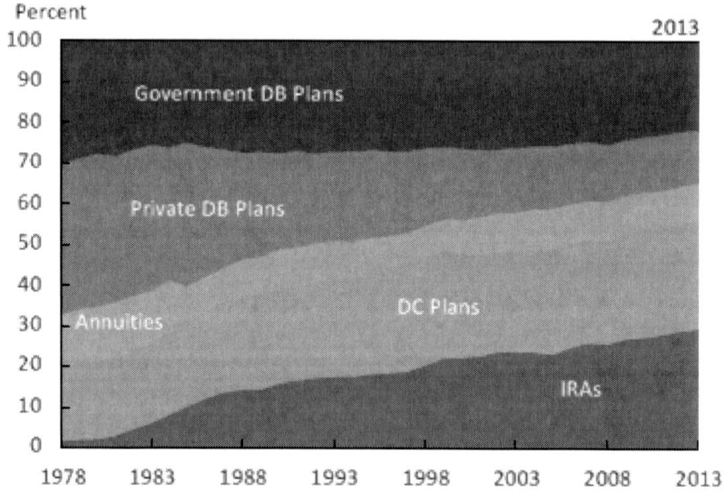

Source: Investment Company Institute.

Figure 1. Retirement Assets by Type, 1978-2013.

This widely discussed shift from traditional pensions to defined contribution plans and IRAs raises important policy issues. In a traditional pension, investment decisions are largely handled by professional managers. In an IRA, investment decisions are almost entirely left to the individual saver. Defined contribution plans, such as 401(k)s, reflect a middle ground where employers may automatically enroll workers in particular default products and may provide workers with access to various forms of advice, but may also provide a large menu of options and nearly unrestricted choice of investment products (Vanguard 2014).

This shift in investment responsibility has coincided with an explosion in the investment options and trading platforms available. The period since 1974 has seen the advent and proliferation of index mutual funds, discount brokerage, exchange-traded funds, online trading, and more. The number and complexity of the products available can make financial decisionmaking difficult (Campbell 2006, Lusardi and Mitchell 2007). Moreover, an abundance of investment options and the way in which investment decisions are framed may challenge financial decisionmaking and lead to worse outcomes for savers (Iyengar et al. 2004, Benartzi et al. 2009). All of these factors in combination have led to an increasing role for financial advice. According to one survey, roughly half of traditional IRA-owning households have a retirement strategy created with the help of a professional financial adviser (Holden and Schrass 2015).

Table 2. Sources of Investment Advice

Adviser	Description	Legal Standard
Registered Investment Advisers (RIAs	Receives compensation in exchange for giving investment advice. May also manage a portfolio for clients.	Fiduciary duty to client, including aduty of loyalty and a duty of care. Must serve the best interest of the client.
Broker Dealers (brokers	Makes trades for a fee or commission. A broker makes trades for a client's account, while a dealer makes trades for his or her own account.	Recommendations must be suitable for a client's investment profile taking into account factors such as age, income, net worth, and investment goals.
Other Potential Sources	Examples include friends, family, bankers, insurance agents, accountants, and lawyers	Standards vary

Retirement savers may obtain investment advice from a range of sources, including two primary groups of professionals: brokers and registered investment advisers (RIAs). Table 2 summarizes select sources of investment advice.[3] In addition to investment and asset allocation recommendations, these advisers may provide overall savings advice, tax planning, estate planning, advice on claiming Social Security, and other services. In this report, we use "financial adviser" broadly to include all kinds of professionals providing advice, not just RIAs.

Two important ways in which advisers differ are (i) the legal and conduct standards that their advice must meet and (ii) the ways in which they are compensated for the advice they provide. For example, advice provided by RIAs must serve the best interest of their clients and satisfy duties of loyalty and care. Brokers' recommendations must be suitable for the client taking into account factors such as age and income. Moreover, only registered investment advisers are permitted to give holistic advice, while brokers are restricted to providing incidental advice (Securities and Exchange Commission (SEC) 2011). However, individual advisers can switch back and forth between the two regimes as they engage in different activities, a practice known as dual hatting. As a result, consumers may not know which legal or conduct regime applies to the advice they are receiving at any moment.

The distinctions between the relevant legal standards are important, but they also interact with an important second difference between advisers: differences in the ways in which they are compensated for the advice provided. The key difference is between those advisers who receive conflicted payments and those who do not. Conflicted payments are payments to the adviser that depend on the actions taken by the advisee. For example, an adviser may receive an annual payment for each dollar invested in certain products. Advisers who do not accept conflicted payments may charge an hourly rate, a percentage of assets, or other similar fees that do not directly depend on the investment decisions made by the client. Advisers may also receive both types of compensation: conflicted payments and payments that do not directly depend on their clients' investment decisions.

Advisers accepting conflicted payments face a conflict of interest because the advice that is best for their own bottom line may not be the advice that is best for their customers' savings. These misaligned interests can arise from a wide range of payment arrangements. Examples include revenue-sharing arrangements and front-end and back-end loads.[4] Table 3 summarizes select forms of conflicted payment arrangements. Advice provided by advisers who accept conflicted payments is referred to as conflicted investment advice. While this report discusses the costs of conflicted investment advice, it is important to keep in mind that many financial advisers hold themselves to high professional standards.

Table 3. Select Types of Payments Generating Conflicts of Interest[5]

Type of Payment	Description of Adviser's Monetary Interest	Potential Consequences
Ongoing revenue-sharing arrangements, including 12b-1 fees	Mutual funds may make ongoing annual payments to advisers based on the advisers' clients' investments, often specified as a percentage of assets. Known by the SEC rule that created them, 12b-1 fees are one example of ongoing revenue-sharing payments.	Creates a financial incentive to direct clients to funds with higher revenue-sharing payments
Front-end sales load, back-end sales load	Mutual funds may charge investors a fee when an investor buys shares (a front-end load) or sells shares (a back-end load). Most or all of this charge is generally passed on to the advisers selling the product.	Creates a financial incentive to steer investors into funds with higher loads and that pass on a larger portion of that load to advisers. Loads also encourage excessive trading as more trades increase load payments.
Sales targets, payouts	Advisers may receive payouts when they achieve certain sales targets. The payout can vary by asset class and product. In some cases, proprietary products receive higher payouts	Creates a financial incentive to recommend trading and selling specific products over others based on the schedule of payouts
Variable commissions	Advisers may receive compensation through commissions for selling individual stocks, insurance products, and other financial products. The amount of the commission can vary across products and asset classes.	Creates a financial incentive to recommend products that generate higher commissions and can encourage excessive trading.

The potential for negative effects of these conflicted payments may be invisible to consumers because they are often unaware of the differences in payment structures and legal standards across advisers and the conflicts they create. Moreover, even when consumers are aware of the differences, they can struggle to know which legal and conduct standard is relevant because advisers can switch between legal and conduct regimes in a given conversation with a client. In surveys, a majority of households reports satisfaction with their advisers and at the same time express confusion and make mistakes about the different titles, legal obligations, and consumer protections that exist in the advice industry (Consumer Financial Protection Bureau (CFPB) 2013, Government Accountability Office (GAO) 2011, Investment Company Institute 1997, SEC 2011). Households also express confusion over the fees that they are charged, reflecting the indirect and sometimes complex pricing of financial advice, which further widens the scope for abuse (Hung et al. 2008).

This report focuses on the impact of conflicted advice as it affects IRA owners. Unique features of the IRA market suggest that IRA investors are particularly vulnerable to conflicted advice. First, few individuals contribute to IRAs directly and, instead, most of the money flowing into these accounts accumulates in employer plans and is then rolled over into an IRA when workers change jobs or retire. In 2012, Americans contributed roughly $30 billion to traditional and Roth IRAs. In the same year, they rolled over more than $300 billion to traditional and Roth IRAs. At the point of rollover, savers are making decisions about large quantities of money relative to the sums involved in other more common financial decisions. Many savers may not have full knowledge about their options or a complete understanding of the detailed regulatory differences between their employer plan and an IRA—most notably that advice to roll money out of the plan into an IRA is generally subject to much lower standards of care than advice received in the plan. Moreover, investment fees in a typical IRA may exceed investment fees in a typical 401(k) according to a series of recent GAO reports (GAO 2009, 2011, 2013). While rolling over balances to an IRA makes financial sense for many people, when doing so incurs meaningfully higher fees, it generally does not.

Second, for many Americans making decisions about their IRA investments will be one of the only times they must confront the full set of investment products available in the marketplace and as such will be one of the most complicated savings decisions they will face in their lifetime.[6] Third, IRA assets are largest for older households who may be more vulnerable to losses due to conflicts than other savers (Agarwal et al. 2009, Lusardi et al. 2009). SEC and CFPB reports have found consumer financial protection abuses that are specifically targeted at elderly households (CFPB 2013, SEC 2007).

While many different financial products provide conflicted payments, the analysis in the next section will largely focus on mutual fund assets. This focus is driven by the existence of high-quality empirical evidence on the issue of conflicts of interest for this subset of the market. As shown in Figure 2, mutual funds accounted for about half of all IRA assets in 2013, or roughly $3.5 trillion.[7] However, to the degree that conflicted payments impose costs outside of mutual funds held in IRAs, the total costs imposed would be larger than the headline estimates in this report.

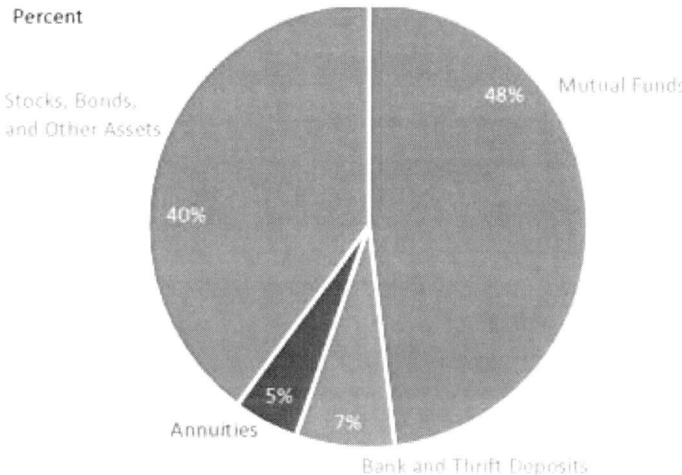

Source: Investment Company Institute.

Figure 2. Allocation of IRA Assets in 2013.

II. The Economic Cost of Conflicted Investment Advice

The efficiency losses arising from economic relationships involving conflicting incentives—that is, scenarios where the best financial outcome for each party in an economic relationship differs and the behavior of one or more parties can only be imperfectly monitored—have been studied extensively in the economics literature. These principal-agent problems have been studied across a range of industries and relationships, including medical care (Arrow 1963), corporate management (Jensen and Meckling 1976), performance management (Holmstrom 1982), and the mutual fund industry (Chen et al. 2013).

This report focuses on quantifying the impact of conflicting incentives in the particular case of financial advisers providing conflicted advice to IRA account holders. To do so, it turns to the empirical literature that examines conflicted payments and investment products characterized by conflicted payments. Numerous empirical studies, summarized in Table 4, identify the many costs that result. Most of the studies in the literature summarize their results in terms of underperformance: the amount by which investment returns for affected products fall short of a suitably-defined comparison group.

In the academic literature, practices vary in whether investment returns are presented before (gross) or after (net) expenses have been taken into account and in exactly which expenses are subtracted before reporting the net return. The Council of Economic Advisers' estimated cost of conflict reflects the impact of conflicted advice on a saver's net return. In the discussion of the empirical evidence in this section, underperformance is often expressed in basis points. Basis points provide a convenient rescaling of percentage points for use when discussing numbers close to 1 percentage point: 1 basis point is equal to 0.01 percentage points, and 100 basis points is 1 percentage point.

This section of the report first reviews the relevant academic literature and then applies the results found in that literature to estimate the effect of conflicted advice on investment returns and the aggregate dollar cost of conflicted investment advice.

The Evidence on Underperformance

A natural place to begin estimating the costs of conflicted investment advice is with a comparison of the investment returns for mutual funds sold through intermediaries and characterized by conflicts of interest with the investment returns for funds sold directly to savers and generally not providing conflicted payments. Importantly, the distinction between these two groups of funds is not identical to the distinction between funds purchased with advice and those without. Savers purchasing funds sold directly to the public may be receiving advice (for example, from a fee-only adviser). Research making this comparison consistently finds that funds characterized by conflicted payments significantly underperform funds sold directly to savers.

Bergstresser et al. (2009) compare the performance of funds sold through intermediaries that tend to offer conflicted payments with that of funds sold directly to savers, where conflicts of interest are significantly weaker. They find that funds sold through intermediaries deliver lower risk-adjusted returns. The researchers examine returns net of operating expenses, but do not include the costs of marketing and selling fund shares such as loads and 12b-1 fees (defined above). Since loads and 12b1 fees are primary sources of compensation for the intermediaries recommending the funds, the authors' finding indicates that it is not merely the cost of paying those intermediaries that leads to underperformance. During the period covered by the study, the annual returns on domestic equity funds sold through intermediaries were 77 basis points lower than the returns of observationally equivalent direct-sold funds. The annual returns on bond funds sold through intermediaries were 90 basis points lower than equivalent direct-sold funds. The authors estimate that this underperformance amounted to $4.6 billion in 2004.[8]

Del Guercio and Reuter (2014) corroborate the result in Bergstresser et al. (2009): direct-sold funds outperform funds sold through intermediaries, a difference they estimate to be 115 basis points per year. Moreover, looking just at funds characterized by conflicted payments, the authors find that actively-managed funds sold through intermediaries, which comprise the vast majority of all funds sold through intermediaries and feature larger conflicted payments, underperform lower-fee, passively-managed funds sold through intermediaries by 112 to 132 basis points per year; this result does not extend to funds that are sold directly to savers. In other words, underperformance among actively-managed funds is limited to the segment of the mutual fund market where the conflicted payments are the largest. The authors conclude that this result "likely reflect[s] an agency conflict between brokers and their clients" as both actively-managed and passively-managed funds sold through intermediaries provide the same portfolio management and advisory services but provide different payments to the adviser.

These first two studies compare investment returns for funds that tend to make conflicted payments with those that do not. One limitation of this type of comparison is that it may incorporate differences other than the presence of conflicted advice between the types of investors purchasing funds through these two sources. For instance, investors purchasing funds through intermediaries may be more risk-averse and less experienced with investing than those buying direct-sold shares from a mutual fund sponsor. Failing to account for such differences may potentially overstate or understate the losses due to conflicts of interest. However, results from another strand of research that is not affected by this limitation find broadly similar patterns.

In one study, Chalmers and Reuter (2014) compare the performance of accounts in an Oregon workplace retirement plan when plan participants lose access to conflicted advisers. They find that participants who would have otherwise used conflicted advisers when available were disproportionately more likely to rely on the plan's default investment options in their absence, and that those default investment options performed better than the portfolios of those receiving conflicted advice. In the authors' words, "brokers significantly increased annual fees, significantly decreased annual after-fee returns, and slightly increased risk-taking relative to the counterfactual portfolio" (that is, the default investment option). The estimated magnitude of underperformance in this study is large: 298 basis points relative to the plan's default investment option. A portion of this large underperformance estimate is explained by a higher exposure to risky assets in broker clients' portfolios at a time when risky assets performed poorly. The authors also estimate underperformance between portfolios selected on the basis of conflicted advice and those that are not after controlling for various measures of investor traits, and find that these portfolios still underperform by approximately 125 basis points. Similarly, researchers examining retail investment advice in Canada and Germany, where the legal regimes differ but advisers also derive substantial compensation from conflicted payments, find that advised accounts underperform by more than 150 basis points (Foerster et al. 2014, Hackethal et al. 2012a).

Conflicted payments can also lead to underperformance as a result of poor timing in investment decisions. Studies that compare the performance of mutual funds do not necessarily capture this effect, which results from the timing of individual investors' decisions to buy and sell. While poor timing in investment decisions, referred to as market mis-timing, exists for reasons other than conflicted payments, conflicted payments can exacerbate the problem as trading strategies with poor timing may generate higher conflicted payments. Friesen and Sapp (2007) estimate that timing issues from all sources could lead to 100 to 200 basis points of annual underperformance and that these losses appear to be larger among a particular group of funds (load funds) offering conflicted payments. Other research also suggests that conflicted advisers often do not steer clients away from excessive trading, another source of investment losses due to poor timing (Hackethal et al. 2012b).

Table 4. Evidence on the Impact of Conflicted Investment Advice

Study	Impact of Conflict	Discussion
Bergstresser et al. (2009)	Lower returns, higher fees	Broker-sold equity, bond, and money market funds underperform corresponding direct-sold funds by 14 to 90 basis points between 1996 and 2004 before accounting for distribution fees that provide compensation for the adviser. Results also show that compensation to advisers is positively associated with net inflows. Study finds little evidence of superior asset allocation or market timing abilities among advisers
Chalmers and Reuter (2014)	Lower returns, higher fees, biased advice	Investors in a university-sponsored retirement plan receiving conflicted advice underperform self-directed investors and a counterfactual targetdate fund by 125 and 298 basis points, respectively. Within the portfolios of those receiving conflicted advice, fund flows are sensitive to the level of fees, with a 50 basis point increase in broker fees corresponding to a 17.2 percentage point higher allocation to the fund with higher fees. Advisers also steer investors away from high-fee funds when those fees do not benefit the advisers.
Christoffersen et al. (2013)	Biased advice, lower returns, higher fees	Between 1993 and 2009, among mutual funds with loads or revenuesharing, higher payments to advisers lead to higher inflows, suggesting that advisers' recommendations are biased by the payments they receive. Net returns are

Table 4. (Continued)

Study	Impact of Conflict	Discussion
		approximately 50 basis points lower for every 100 basis points of loads that are shared with advisers.
Del Guercio and Reuter (2014)	Lower returns, higher fees	Actively managed broker-sold mutual funds earn returns 112 to 132 basis points lower than passively managed broker-sold funds, after accounting for distribution fees that provide compensation for the adviser. The authors conclude that this underperformance likely reflects an agency conflict between advisers and their clients.
Foerster et al. (2014)	Lower returns, higher fees, inappropriate risktaking, advice is not customized	Among Canadian investors, advised portfolios primarily relying on conflicted advice pay 170 basis points more than a lifecycle fund but experience worse market timing and fund selection. Advisers encourage additional risk-taking, but the gain in returns is offset by the higher fees charged by the adviser, leaving the investor with lower risk-adjusted performance than with a lifecycle fund or passive index.
Friesen and Sapp (2007)	Market mis-timing	Investors in load funds experience larger losses (194 basis points) from market mis-timing than those in no-load funds (96 basis points). Losses for both groups are relative to a buy-and-hold strategy.
GAO (2011)	Inappropriate rollovers	In a review of the market, certain advisers' compensation can range from $6,000 to $9,000 if an employer-based plan participant were to purchase an IRA but only $50 to

Study	Impact of Conflict	Discussion
		$100 if the same participant were to remain in the plan.
Hackethal et al. (2012a)	Lower returns, higher turnover	Clients of a German brokerage and a German bank receiving advice from advisers primarily compensated through conflicted payments earn lower net returns not justified by reduced risk. Clients' accounts also exhibited higher turnover.
Hackethal et al. (2012b	Excessive trading, biased advice, higher fees	Investors receiving conflicted advice from a German retail bank between 2005 and 2007 trade more heavily, are more likely to purchase "incentivized" products (e.g. funds with higher loads), and generate higher bank revenues, holding investor characteristics, including financial sophistication, constant.
Mullainathan et al. (2012)	Market mis-timing, higher fees, inappropriate diversification, asset misallocation	In 284 mystery shopper visits to financial advisers, a majority of advisers recommend investment strategies that are in line with their financial interests, such as return chasing and buying actively managed funds. Moreover, advisers steer clients away from low-fee, passively managed portfolios toward higher-fee products

The studies reviewed so far in this section provide a consistently negative view of the risk-adjusted, post-fee performance of portfolios invested according to conflicted advice but they do not directly link the extent of the underperformance to the magnitude of the conflicted payments. To establish the direct link between conflicts of interest and underperformance, we turn to another set of results in the academic literature. In one study, researchers connected the payments an intermediary receives for selling a particular mutual fund to underperformance (Christoffersen et al. 2013). Comparing data on flows and performance for mutual funds that have unusually high or low payments to intermediaries, the researchers find that inflows are larger for funds with unusually high payments and smaller for those with unusually low payments. Put somewhat differently, if two funds appear otherwise identical but one shares a higher portion of load payments with advisers, the amount of money flowing into that fund will tend to be higher. The authors also find that higher revenue-sharing payments lead to greater inflows. These results provide direct evidence that two important sources of conflicts—namely, load payments and revenue sharing—bias investment recommendations.

Further, the authors find that unusually high or low load-sharing payments lead to unusually low or high performance, respectively. That is, funds with unusually high payments to intermediaries tend to generate unusually low returns.[9] In particular, the average conflicted payment to certain advisers in their data "corresponds to a 1.13% reduction in annual performance" after fees.

The finding that conflicted payments drive investment decisions is corroborated by evidence presented in Chalmers and Reuter (2014). The researchers find that fund flows are sensitive to the level of fees more generally, concluding that a 50 basis point increase in adviser fees corresponds to a 17.2 percentage point higher allocation to the fund. This study also finds evidence that advisers steer investors away from high-fee funds when those fees do not benefit the adviser.

The studies discussed to this point analyze the impact of conflicted payments on mutual fund flows and performance. An alternative perspective on advice can be obtained by examining how advisers treat individuals and assessing the degree to which their recommendations are motivated by the payments they receive. In a mystery shopper study, researchers sent hypothetical investors to financial advisers largely reliant on conflicted payments for their compensation to investigate the type of advice provided (Mullainathan et al. 2012). The mystery shoppers presented four portfolios to advisers: a return-chasing portfolio, an employer stock portfolio, a diversified low-fee portfolio, and a cash portfolio. The study finds that advisers recommend a change to the current investment strategy in about 60 percent of cases when the client had a return-chasing portfolio and in about 85 percent of cases in which the client had a diversified low-fee portfolio. The authors conclude that advisers "seem to support strategies that result in more transactions and higher management fees," even when clients appear to hold the optimal portfolio.

In the U.S. retirement system, a particularly important financial decision occurs when employees who participate in a workplace retirement plan change jobs or retire and must decide what to do with their existing savings. The options at this point typically include leaving their savings in the current plan, rolling them over into a new employer's plan, or rolling them over into an IRA. However, advisers may recommend inappropriate rollovers to plan participants to collect fees for managing the assets. According to a recent GAO report, certain advisers could earn $6,000 to $9,000 if a plan participant were to purchase an IRA but only $50 to $100 if the same participant were to invest within the employer plan (GAO 2011). Recent analyses have found that plan participants are frequently encouraged to roll over funds to an IRA with minimal knowledge of the participant's financial situation, without acknowledging other options available, and without offering significant discussion of fees (GAO 2013).

The Effect of Conflicted Advice on Investment Returns

As discussed above and seen in Table 4, academic research identifies several ways in which conflicted advice affects investment performance. Because the studies reviewed in this report examine different, partially overlapping aspects of conflict and because they vary in the extent to which their effects are directly attributed to conflict, it would not be appropriate to simply sum or average the estimates to obtain a single overall estimate of the effect of conflicted advice. But taken together, the evidence suggests that conflicted advice leads to underperformance of roughly 100 basis points per year. Here, we outline the various considerations that lead us to this estimate.

Our approach starts from a study that directly examines the relationship between payments to advisers and performance. Christoffersen et al. (2013) conclude that the magnitude of losses from conflict corresponding to the fund with the average load-sharing payment is 113 basis points, which is in line with our estimate. However, whether this estimate is a good indicator of conflict-driven underperformance today depends on the relative magnitudes of at least three adjustments that may either push the estimate higher or lower. First, average loads may be somewhat lower today than the average during the period studied in the paper (1993 to 2009), which would lead us to adjust the underperformance estimate down. Second, this estimate does not factor in the direct impact of the additional load payment the investor incurs as a result of the recommendation to invest in funds with higher loads, which would lead to an upward adjustment. Third, the authors estimate underperformance for the first year in which the funds are purchased rather than underperformance for every year that the saver holds the fund. Adjusting for this detail would increase or decrease the underperformance estimate depending on whether the effect grows or decays in subsequent years. While the literature provides little formal guidance on this specific question, the authors control for cyclical fluctuations that might lead their underperformance estimate to differ depending on business cycle conditions. In addition, studies that estimate underperformance in portfolios, where a fund's performance can be tracked beyond the first year of ownership, find annual estimates of underperformance over time that are consistent with the first-year effect (Hackethal et al. 2012b, Chalmers and Reuter 2014, Foerster et al. 2014). Both of these explanations provide suggestive evidence that the one-year estimate of underperformance in Christoffersen et al. (2013) is a reasonable approximation for the persistent effect. Taking all three of these adjustments into consideration leads us to conclude that 100 basis points is a plausible estimate around which to center the magnitude of underperformance.

An alternative approach would build up the estimate from separate estimates for each of the ways conflicted investment advice can lead to underperformance: excessive fees, excessive trading, market mis-timing, and so forth. However, there is insufficient precision in the literature to separately estimate each of these sources of underperformance in such a calculation—although the individual estimates cited above support an aggregate estimate of 100 basis points in that many of the individual estimates in the literature are 100 basis points or higher.

As with any attempt to assign a specific value to an unobservable quantity, there is uncertainty in this estimated cost of conflict. For example, if a large fraction of market mis-timing reflects the impact of conflicted advice, the cost could be larger. If the impact of unusually high or low conflicted payments on performance (the basis for the Christoffersen et al. (2013) analysis) differs systematically from the impact of expected differences in conflicted payments, the cost of conflict could be either over or understated.

How Conflicted Advice Erodes Retirement Savings

The definition of underperformance used in this report is broad and encompasses a wide range of channels through which returns can suffer, including high fees, high trading costs, poor market timing, and increased risk exposure without increased returns. Because these sources of underperformance reflect a mix of implicit and explicit costs that may not appear on any account statement, it can be difficult to see how they reduce the returns a worker earns on his retirement savings.

This box provides a simplified example to illustrate what underperformance means in practice.

Consider two potential options for a worker who has recently changed jobs: leaving her 401(k) balance in the old plan or rolling over to an IRA. (In many cases, the worker could also choose to roll over the balance to a retirement plan at the new job. For simplicity, this example ignores this option as well as the option to withdraw the balance from the account.)

Suppose the worker's previous employer ran a large 401(k) plan with several low-cost investment options, and the worker was invested in an index fund holding a mix of stocks and bonds. Suppose further that the expected return for the fund's portfolio before accounting for any expenses is 6.5 percent. In practice, it is not possible for the worker to earn this return because it is the return that would be earned if the fund didn't need to pay anyone to make trades, manage customer service, process employee contributions to the plan, and so on. The trading costs for index funds tend to be quite low; this example assumes they lower the saver's expected return by 5 basis points. The fund's management and operating expenses reduce the returns by another 20 basis points. Finally, the costs of administering the 401(k) plan itself reduce returns by another 25 basis points. Altogether, these expenses reduce the return by 50 basis points.

Thus, each year that the worker holds this investment, she can expect to earn 6.5 percent minus 0.5 percent for a net gain of 6.0 percent (see Table). Of course, in any particular year, returns may be higher or lower depending on the performance of the market.

	401(k)	Recommended IRA
Portfolio's gross return	6.50%	6.50%
- Trading costs	0.05%	0.20%
- Mutual fund expenses	0.20%	1.30%
- 401(k) plan expenses	0.25%	0.00%
Saver's net return	6.00%	5.00%

Now suppose the worker receives a recommendation to roll over her balance to an IRA and invest in a higher cost mutual fund with an investment strategy that involves more frequent trading. This type of recommendation can arise because the person making the recommendation receives higher compensation if the worker rolls over her balance to an IRA than if she keeps her funds in her 401(k).

However, unless the fund involves a significantly different risk profile than the index fund, the expected return will likely be quite similar.

This example simplifies and assumes the IRA investment matches the risk characteristics of the 401(k) investment and earns an identical expected return before accounting for any costs. Yet the fund's frequent trading strategy results in significantly higher trading costs, reducing returns by 20 basis points rather than 5. In addition, the mutual fund's management and operating expenses are 130 basis points, up from 20. However, in the IRA the worker would no longer need to pay the 401(k) plan management fees, which reduced returns by 25 basis points. In combination, the costs for the IRA investment reduce earnings by 150 basis points annually. Thus, each year the saver holds this investment she can expect to earn 5 percent.

In this example, conflicted advice reduces the expected return on a saver's investment each year from 6 percent to 5 percent. Over time, reduced annual returns add up to significant reductions in a saver's potential retirement savings. Suppose the worker's rollover occurred at age 45 and she expects to retire at 65. The 1 percentage point reduction in the expected annual return leads to a reduction in the expected value of her savings from this account at age 65 of 17 percent.

Lower returns likewise reduce the value of accumulated savings in the retirement years. For a saver who plans to take withdrawals over a 30-year period (*beginning* immediately), the lower return resulting from conflicted advice will require her to reduce the annual withdrawals from the account by 12 percent compared to what she could have withdrawn each year absent conflicts of interest.[a] Alternatively, if she chooses to withdraw the amount that could have been withdrawn each year when earning the higher return, she would run out of money more than five years earlier.

These losses in retirement come on top of the losses in the pre-retirement period for workers with a mid-career rollover. For the saver in this example who rolls over her 401(k) balance at 45, the combined effect of a 17 percent loss leading up to retirement and a 12 percent loss after retirement is an overall loss of more than 25 percent. That is, as a result of conflicted investment advice, the feasible retirement withdrawals for this saver fall by more than 25 percent compared to what would have been possible with unconflicted advice.

[a] Withdrawal computations assume constant inflation-adjusted withdrawals and an inflation rate of 2 percent.

The Dollar Cost of Conflicted Investment Advice

Translating the effect of conflicted advice on investment returns into a dollar cost requires an estimate of the value of assets invested according to conflicted advice. We can then multiply the estimated value of affected assets by the effect of conflict on investment returns to obtain the total dollar cost of conflict.

Implementing this straightforward computation, however, is complicated by the number of different ways in which advice can be delivered, the methodological differences across empirical studies, and the limitations of the publicly available data. Systematic, quantitative evidence on the effects of conflict is richest for mutual funds. As a result, a conservative approach would apply the effect of conflicted advice on investment returns obtained above only to a pool of mutual fund assets affected by conflicts of interest. A less conservative approach would apply the cost of conflicted advice obtained for mutual funds to all assets affected by conflicts of interest, using the underperformance among mutual funds as indicative of the effect across investment products.

We identify three potential estimates of IRA assets subject to conflicted investment advice. The first—and narrowest—estimate corresponds to mutual funds with loads in IRAs. While using load funds as an indicator of conflicted payments is imperfect, as such funds can waive loads for certain investors and a saver could simply choose to invest in such a fund even without receiving advice, it almost certainly underestimates the pool of assets affected by conflicted advice by excluding an extremely large range of products, including variable annuities and no-load funds, that could be recommended on the basis of conflicted payments. We estimate the value of load funds in IRAs by multiplying the share of load funds among non-institutional mutual fund assets at the end of 2013 by the total value of mutual fund assets in IRAs. This yields an estimate of $1.05 trillion.[10]

Table 5. Estimates of IRA Assets Affected by Conflicted Investment Advice

	IRA Assets Affected	Asset Composition
Low	$1.05 trillion	Value of load mutual funds in IRAs
Middle	$1.66 trillion	Value of load mutual funds and annuities in IRAs
High	$3.26 trillion	Value of advised IRA assets

The second estimate of IRA assets invested according to conflicted investment advice is the combination of load funds and variable annuity mutual funds in IRAs. (Variable annuities often provide conflicted payments such as differential commissions and revenue-sharing payments.) This estimate captures a larger share of potentially affected assets and maintains a focus on the mutual fund products that were the focus of the empirical research reviewed above. We estimate this pool in the same manner as the pool above, taking the share of load funds and variable annuity mutual funds among non-institutional mutual fund assets and multiplying by the value of mutual fund assets in IRAs. This yields an estimate of $1.66 trillion.

The third estimate of IRA assets invested according to conflicted investment advice is a conservative estimate of IRA assets for which individuals receive any advice. We compute this by multiplying the value of IRA assets by the share of traditional IRA owners who consulted a professional financial adviser when creating a retirement strategy.[11] This yields an estimate of $3.26 trillion. While this estimate likely underestimates the value of IRA assets invested according to professional advice, as large accounts are likely disproportionately advised, it likely overestimates the value invested according to conflicted advice as some advice does not involve conflicts of interest. Moreover, applying the estimated cost of conflict in this manner requires extending results obtained from analysis of mutual fund performance to many other kinds of assets. Despite these limitations of the analysis, it is important to understand the potential cost of conflict across all assets rather than assuming that conflicts of interest do not affect assets other than mutual funds. Finally, as this report focuses on quantifying the cost of conflicted advice on IRA savings, the estimates are inherently conservative as they exclude a substantial fraction of all savings.

Each of these three approaches has advantages and disadvantages. Focusing on load funds in IRAs limits attention to a set of investments most closely related to those analyzed in the academic research reviewed above. Moreover, it restricts attention to a pool of assets highly likely to be invested according to conflicted advice. And, by virtue of excluding all assets other than load funds, it likely underestimates the relevant pool of assets even though some load fund assets may not be subject to conflict. However, this conservative approach likely substantially understates the total cost of conflict by ignoring conflicted advice to invest in other products. The second estimate's focus on load funds and variable annuity mutual funds remains close to the subject of academic studies but encompasses a somewhat wider array of products. Finally, the full set of IRA assets subject to advice likely overstates the cost of conflicted advice for IRA owners as some of the advice may be provided by advisers who do not receive conflicted payments. Moreover, it applies empirical evidence obtained from studies primarily of mutual funds to a context where it may be less relevant. However, as noted above, the costs of conflicted advice extend beyond the IRA market considered here.

Applying the estimated effect of conflict on investment returns to the intermediate estimate of affected assets yields an annual cost of conflict for retirement savers of $17 billion. Importantly, while the precise magnitude of the underperformance depends on the point estimates chosen, the scale of the loss does not. Even if the effect of conflict on investment returns is half as large, retirement savers are losing $8.5 billion per year. On the other hand, if the pool of affected assets is better approximated by the high estimate above, retirement savers are losing $33 billion per year.

Is the Current System the Only Way for Americans with Modest Savings to Obtain Advice?

This analysis concludes that conflicted advice costs Americans about $17 billion in foregone retirement earnings each year. The costly effects of conflicted advice may be particularly relevant for Americans with modest retirement savings, as historically they have relied on types of advice often subject to conflicts. Due to these patterns, some observers have asserted that advising structures using conflicted payments are the only way that savers with lower balances can obtain advice and that without such advice the adequacy of their retirement savings would suffer. This argument, however, falls short in multiple ways and overlooks channels that could provide high-quality, conflict-free advice to moderate-income savers at the same cost as conflicted advising structures.

First, advisers can provide the same quality of advice while receiving non-conflict-based payments as they can when receiving a payment of equal amount based in conflict. The cost of advice depends primarily on the resources necessary to provide it—the adviser's time, IT infrastructure, and other inputs—rather than the form of the adviser's compensation. Thus, an adviser receiving payment through non-conflicted structures should be able to provide advice at the same cost as an adviser receiving conflicted payments, as long as the inputs in time and infrastructure are equal.

If advisers serving moderate-income Americans can remain profitable regardless of whether they receive conflicted or non-conflicted compensation, one would expect the number of advisers working with lower-balance savers to remain the same regardless of whether conflict-based payment systems remain in use.

Second, the prevalence of conflicted payments today may actually interfere with low-balance savers' ability to get advice. Ongoing developments in the financial industry are sharply reducing the cost of advice, but it may be difficult for new entrants providing quality, unconflicted, low-cost advice to compete on price when other advice erroneously appears to be free. Therefore the prevalence of hidden fees and conflicted payments may make it more difficult for low-cost, high-quality alternatives to compete on a level playing field, reducing moderate-income Americans' available options for inexpensive advice. As just one example, new approaches to advice that exploit technological advances are allowing firms to offer personalized advice at costs well below those of traditional advice.

Finally, savers with modest balances today tend to become savers with larger balances tomorrow. According to the Employee Benefit Research Institute, more than 60 percent of IRA contributors in 2010 contributed in at least one of the next two years and nearly 40 percent contributed in every year from 2010 to 2012 (Copeland 2014). A significant motivator for the services provided to low-balance customers today is likely their potential to become higher balance customers in the future. Financial advisers have strong incentives to work with lower-balance savers regardless of whether using conflicted or non-conflicted payment structures.

III. Alternative Explanations for Underperformance

The previous section reviews a range of studies that quantify the costs of conflicted investment advice in terms of underperformance. Some of the most compelling studies examine conflicted payments and advice directly, such as the study by Christoffersen et al. (2013) that finds higher conflicted payments drive increased investment in mutual funds and correspond to underperformance of such funds. Other studies provide evidence that mutual funds that tend to make conflicted payments underperform those that do not. While conflicted payments are a logical explanation for the underperformance identified in this second group of studies, other alternative explanations have been advanced for the finding. In this section, we explore two alternative explanations. Generally speaking, the support in the literature for these alternative explanations is unsatisfying. As a result, although we acknowledge the possibility that factors other than conflicts of interest could be at play, we do not find enough compelling evidence or justification to challenge our conclusion that advisers' conflicts of interest are quantitatively significant and erode households' retirement assets by billions of dollars each year. Moreover, even if these alternative explanations are a factor in generating underperformance in funds that typically make conflicted payments, they would not explain why atypically high conflicted payments generate additional flows and additional underperformance.

Is Underperformance the Fair Price of Advice and Other Intangible Benefits?

Advisers deserve fair compensation for their services. In many cases, their earnings are derived from conflicted payments. Thus, one alternative explanation for underperformance among funds offering conflicted payments is that this underperformance merely reflects the necessary and reasonable compensation for advisers. However, much of the research is careful to exclude fees used to compensate advisers from their underperformance calculation. For example, the baseline results reported in Bergstresser et al. (2009) report underperformance before fees used to provide adviser compensation are taken into account. Thus, it is unlikely that the underperformance reflects the fair price of advice.

Relatedly, given the existence of underperformance in these funds, some question whether investors select such funds for intangible benefits provided by the funds or the advisers that recommend them. However, other research results raise doubts about this explanation. For example, studies find that households are mostly unaware of their advisers' conflicts and compensation arrangements, suggesting they have not built an assessment of those conflicts into their selection of the adviser (Malmendier and Shanthikumar 2007, Mullainathan et al. 2012, SEC 2011). Also, in an experimental setting where fees are made salient, Choi et al. (2010) conclude that investors are unlikely to buy high-fee funds for the bundled services they provide. Lastly, studies document how, in many consumer finance contexts, the opaque pricing of financial products can create opportunities for potential abuses, particularly affecting elderly consumers.[12] All of these considerations suggest that the opaque and complex pricing structures are likely to pose challenges for households.

Does Underperformance Reflect the Characteristics of Households Receiving Conflicted Advice Rather than Conflict Itself?

Households differ in their financial characteristics, such as net worth and income; their knowledge of personal finance; and the competing demands on their time. Customers purchasing mutual funds characterized by conflicted payments differ modestly from those purchasing mutual funds directly along certain dimensions, such as income and education (Bergstresser et al. 2009). If correlated with their investment needs or abilities, these differences could lead to underperformance among funds characterized by conflicted payments. However, as noted in the original paper, while these differences could easily lead to differences in willingness to pay for advice (in either direction), it is not clear why they would necessarily lead to differences in underperformance after accounting for the fees that provide compensation for the adviser.

Households from all backgrounds fall subject to common behavioral biases, such as over-confidence, over-optimism, and loss aversion. These biases often lead to lower investment returns because they lead households to (i) trade excessively by seeking active management or chasing returns, (ii) sell winning investments while holding losing investments, (iii) overweight past returns, or (iv) underdiversify.[13] If households affected by these biases disproportionately hold funds characterized by conflicted payments, it may be the case that these biases, rather than the conflicts of interest among financial advisers, lead to the underperformance.

This second possibility is less directly addressed by papers that focus solely on underperformance at the fund level. However, turning to the other results reviewed above that directly examine financial advice provides insight. For example, Mullainathan et al. (2012) find that in a sample of advisers who predominantly rely on conflicted payments for their income, advisers often recommend substantial changes to portfolios that currently follow best practices and are less likely to recommend changes to portfolios that do not follow best practices when doing so would likely reduce their earnings. This finding raises significant doubts about the extent to which conflicted advice is serving as a brake on behavioral biases.

Do Mandated Disclosures Provide a Solution?

Mandated disclosures are a common regulatory tool for promoting the transparency and comprehension of consumer financial products. Despite their ubiquity, when used to inform savers of the conflicts of interest between them and their advisers, the effects of disclosure by itself are limited and, in many cases, lead to harm and weaker consumer protections. Indeed, many financial advisers already provide disclosures and the evidence discussed in this report suggests that they are not highly effective. Here, we briefly explore some of the challenges with disclosures in the market for financial advice.[a]

Perhaps most importantly, current disclosure practices for IRAs and retail financial investment products lack salience. They are often discussed in fine print sections using legal language or other terms whose meaning may be opaque. It should not be surprising then that investors seldom read financial disclosures, viewing them as meaningless, and therefore do not become informed by them (ICI 2006). Moreover, when disclosures are presented at the point of sale, as is common in many financial transactions, it is often too late for the disclosure to influence investors' decisions, even for financially sophisticated individuals.

Even if disclosures are highly salient, design challenges remain. Research suggests that disclosures are most effective when they simultaneously satisfy three criteria: accessibility, accuracy, and relevance, and it is difficult to simultaneously satisfy these three objectives. Nevertheless, the need to do so is especially acute when the amount of information a consumer needs is vast and when products are complex, as is the case with IRA investments. Because individuals can only process a limited amount of information at one time, it is easy to overload them with too much information, which necessitates hard choices and tradeoffs in what should be disclosed. Given how differently individuals process financial information, the disclosure design must recognize that the same information can easily be interpreted differently by different types of individuals.

Finally, in practice, disclosures of conflicts of interest can actually backfire (Cain et al. 2005, Loewenstein et al. 2011).

Research in behavioral economics and psychology demonstrates that when advisers disclose their conflicts, they may be more willing to pursue their own interest over those of their clients and thus give worse advice. Advisees may interpret the disclosure as a sign of honesty and become more likely to follow their advisers' biased advice.

[a] For a fuller discussion of mandated disclosures, see Ben-Shahar and Schneider (2011).

International Policy Changes to Mitigate Conflicted Advice

Several countries have recently enacted regulations to mitigate conflicts of interest for retail financial products. The United Kingdom and Australia both banned payments from product providers to advisers and increased disclosure requirements. The European Union Markets in Financial Instruments Directive 2 (MiFID 2), scheduled to take effect by early 2017, proposes to ban conflicted payments for certain advisers and requires policies and procedures to ensure that any advisers who accept conflicted payments are properly incentivized to serve clients' interests.[a] The table below summarizes recent international policy changes to address conflicted advice in select countries.[b]

Australia[c]	Banned payments from product providers and conflicted remuneration payments for retail investments and created a statutory duty for advisers to act in the best interest of their
Canada	New regulations, implementation of which began in 2014, require much greater transparency about the direct and indirect costs to the client for each account and details on adviser compensation by clients and product providers.
India	Banned all front loads for mutual fund products beginning in 2009. Implemented heightened requirements to disclose the value and justification for any commission payments to advisers.
Italy	Banned commissions for discretionary portfolio management services beginning in 2007.
Germany	Increased disclosures about the cost of advice and whether advisers are compensated solely through client fees or by payments from service providers.
The Netherlands	Banned all payments by a product issuer to an adviser relating to advice beginning in 2013. The ban applies to investment, insurance, and mortgage and protection (annuity) products.

United Kingdomd	Banned conflicted payments, increased education and credentialing standards, and required advisers to disclose whether they make recommendations from a restricted menu of products or across all products beginning in 2013.

[a] European Parliament (2014).

[b] Information in the table below comes from BlackRock (2014) unless otherwise noted.

[c] Australian Securities & Investment Commission (2015).

[d] Financial Conduct Authority (2014).

CONCLUSION

This report examines the evidence on the cost of conflicted investment advice and its effects on Americans' retirement savings, with a focus on IRAs. The Council of Economic Advisers' survey of the evidence suggests that conflicted advice reduces investment returns by roughly 1 percentage point for savers receiving that advice. In the aggregate, such savers hold about $1.7 trillion of IRA assets. Thus, we estimate the aggregate annual cost of conflicted advice is about $17 billion each year.

The conclusions of this report are based on a careful review of the relevant academic literature but, as with any such analysis, are subject to uncertainty. However, this uncertainty should not mask the essential finding of this report: conflicted advice leads to large and economically meaningful costs for Americans' retirement savings. Even a far more conservative estimate of the investment losses due to conflicted advice, such as half of a percentage point, would yield annual losses of more than $8 billion. On the other hand, if conflicted advice affects a larger portion of IRA assets than the $1.7 trillion considered here—or if the estimate were extended to other forms of retirement savings—the total annual cost would exceed $17 billion.

REFERENCES

Agarwal, Sumit, John C. Driscoll, Xavier Gabaix, and David Laibson. 2009. "The Age of Reason: Financial Decisions over the Lifecycle with Implications for Regulation." *Brookings Papers on Economic Activity* 2: 51-117.

Arrow, Kenneth J. 1963. "Uncertainty and the Welfare Economics of Medical Care." *The American Economic Review* 53(5): 941-973.

Australian Securities & Investment Commission. 2015. "FOFA - Background and implementation." Australian Securities & Investment Commission. < http://asic.gov.au/regulatory-resources/financial-services/future-of-financial-advice-reforms/fofa-background-and-implementation/>.

Barber, Brad, and Terrance Odean. 2000. "Trading is Hazardous to Your Wealth: The Common Stock Investment Performance of Individual Investors." Journal of Finance LV(2): 773-806. Barber, Brad, and Terrance Odean. 2001. "Boys will be Boys: Gender, Overconfidence, and Common Stock Investment." *Quarterly Journal of Economics* 116(1): 261-292.

Barber, Brad, and Terrance Odean. 2002. "Online Investors: Do the Slow Die First?" *Review of Financial Studies* 15(2): 455-487.

Barber, Brad, and Terrance Odean. 2013. "The Behavior of Individual Investors." *Handbook of the Economic of Finance* 2(B): 1533-1570.

Benartzi, Shlomo, and Richard H. Thaler. 2001. "Naive Diversification Strategies in Defined Contribution Saving Plans." *American Economic Review* 91(1): 79-98.

Benartzi, Shlomo, Ehud Peleg, and Richard H. Thaler. 2009. "Choice Architecture and Retirement Saving Plans." In Eldar Shafir (Ed.). The Behavioral Foundations of Policy. *Russell Sage Foundation and Princeton University Press.*

Ben-Shahar, Omri, and Carl E. Schneider. 2011. "The failure of mandated disclosure." University of Pennsylvania Law Review, 647-749.

Bergstresser, Daniel, John Chalmers, and Peter Tufano. 2009. "Assessing the Costs and Benefits of Brokers in the Mutual Fund Industry." The Review of Financial Studies 22(10): 4129-4156.

BlackRock. 2014. "The Changing Face of European Distribution: A Better Financial Future for Savers?" BlackRock ViewPoints. http://www.blackrock.com/corporate/enbr/literature/whitepaper/viewpoint-european-distribution-may-2014.pdf.

Cain, Daylian M., George Loewenstein, and Don A. Moore. 2005. "The Dirt on Coming Clean: Perverse Effects of Disclosing Conflicts of Interest." *The Journal of Legal Studies* 34 (1): 1-25.

Calvet, Laurent E., John Y. Campbell, and Paolo Sodini. 2007. "Down or Out: Assessing the Welfare Costs of Household Investment Mistakes." *Journal of Political Economy* 115(October): 707- 747.

Campbell, John Y. 2006. "Household Finance." *Journal of Finance* 61(4): 1553-1604.

Chalmers, John, and Jonathan Reuter. 2014. "What is the Impact of Financial Advisers on Retirement Portfolio Choices and Outcomes?" National Bureau of Economic Research Working Paper w18158. https://www2.bc.edu/jonathan-reuter/research/ORP_201405.pdf.

Chen, Joseph, Harrison Hong, Wenxi Jiang, and Jeffrey D. Kubik. 2013. "Outsourcing Mutual Fund Management: Firm Boundaries, Incentives, and Performance." *The Journal of Finance* 68 (2): 523-558.

Choi, James J., David Laibson, and Brigitte C. Madrian. 2010. "Why does the law of one price fail? An experiment on index mutual funds." *Review of Financial Studies* 23 (4): 1405-1432.

Choi, James J., David Laibson, and Brigitte C. Madrian. 2011. "$100 bills on the sidewalk: Suboptimal investment in 401(k) plans." *Review of Economics and Statistics* 93(3): 748-763.

Christoffersen, Susan E.K., Richard Evans, and David K. Musto. 2013. "What Do Consumers' Fund Flows Maximize? Evidence from Their Brokers' Incentives." *Journal of Finance* 68(1): 201-235.

Consumer Financial Protection Bureau (CFPB). 2013. "Senior Designations for Financial Advisers: Reducing Consumer Confusion and Risks." http://files.consumerfinance.gov/f/201304_CFPB_OlderAmericans_Report.pdf.

Copeland, Craig. 2014. "Individual Retirement Account Balances, Contributions, and Rollovers, 2012; With Longitudinal Results 2010–2012: The EBRI IRA Database." Employee Benefit Research Institute 339. http://www.ebri.org/pdf/briefspdf/ebri_ib_399_may14.iras.pdf.

Del Guercio, Diane, and Jonathan Reuter. 2014. "Mutual Fund Performance and the Incentive to Generate Alpha." *The Journal of Finance* 69: 1673-1704.

Engel, Kathleen C., and Patricia A. McCoy. 2002. "A Tale of Three Markets: The Law and Economics of Predatory Lending." *Texas Law Review* 80 (6): 1255.

European Parliament. 2014. "MEPs vote laws to regulate financial markets and curb high-frequency trading." Committee on Economic and Monetary Affairs. http://www.europarl.europa.eu/pdfs/news/expert/infopress/ 2014 0411IPR43438/20140411IP R43438_en.pdf

Financial Conduct Authority. 2014. "Retail Distribution Review (RDR)." London. Accessed February 19, 2015. http://www.fca.org.uk/firms/firm-types/sole-advisers/rdr#

Financial Industry Regulatory Authority (FINRA). 2013. "Report on Conflict of Interest." http://www.finra.org/web/groups/industry/@ip/@reg/ @ guide/documents/industry/p35997 1.pdf.

Foerster, Stephen, Juhani T. Linnainmaa, Brian T. Melzer, and Alessandro Previtero. 2014. "Retail Financial Advice: Does One Size Fit All?" National Bureau of Economic Research Working Paper 20712.

Friesen, Geoffrey C., and Travis RA Sapp. 2007. "Mutual Fund Flows and Investor Returns: An Empirical Examination of Fund Investor Timing Ability." *Journal of Banking and Finance* 31(9): 2796-2816.

Government Accountability Office (GAO). 2009. "Conflicts of Interest Can Affect Defined Benefit and Defined Contribution Plans." GAO-09-503T. http://www.gao.gov/assets/ 130/122042.pdf. —. 2011. "401(K) Plans: Improved Regulation Could Better Protect Participants from Conflicts of Interest." GAO-11-119. http://www.gao.gov/assets/320/315369.html.

—. 2013. "401(K) Plans: Labor and IRS Could Improve the Rollover Process for Participants." GAO-13- 30. http://www.gao.gov/assets/660/ 652881 .pdf.

Hackethal, Andreas, Michael Haliassos, and Tullio Jappelli. 2012a. "Financial Advisers: A Case of Babysitters?" *Journal of Banking and Finance* 36(2): 509-524.

Hackethal, Andreas, Roman Inderst, and Steffen Meyer. 2012b. "Trading on Advice." University of Frankfurt. Available at SSRN 1701777.

Holden, Sarah, and Daniel Schrass. 2015. "The Role of IRAs in the U.S. Households' Saving for Retirement, 2014." ICI Research Perspective 21(1). http://www.ici.org/pdf/per21-01.pdf.

Holmstrom, Bengt. 1982. "Moral hazard in teams." The Bell Journal of Economics 13(2): 324-340. Howat, John, and Linda Reid. 2007. "Compensation Practices for Retail Sale of Mutual Funds: the Need for Transparency and Disclosure." *Fordham Journal of Corporate and Financial Law* 12(4): 687-91.

Hung, Angela A., Noreen Clancy, Jeff Dominitz, Eric Talley, Claude Berrebi, and Farrukh Suvankulov. 2008. Investor and Industry Perspectives on Investment Advisers and Broker-Dealers. RAND Corporation.

Infogroup/ORC. 2010. "Elder Investment Fraud and Financial Exploitation A Survey Conducted for Investor Protection Trust." Investor Protection Trust. Washington, DC. http://www.investorprotection.org/downloads/ EIFFE_Survey_Report.pdf

Investment Company Institute (ICI). 1997. "Understanding Shareholders' Use of Information and Advisers." Washington, DC. http://www.ici.org/pdf/rpt_undstnd_share.pdf

—. 2006. "Understanding Investor Preferences for Mutual Fund Information." Washington, DC. http://www.ici.org/pdf/rpt_06_inv_prefs_full.pdf.

—. 2014. "2014 Investment Company Fact Book: A Review of Trends and Activities in the U.S. Investment Company Industry." 54th Edition. http://www.ici.org/pdf/2014_factbook.pdf.

Iyengar, Sheena S., Gur Huberman, and Wei Jiang. 2004. "How Much Choice is Too Much? Contributions to 401(k) retirement plans." In Mitchell, Olivia S., and Stephen Utkus (Ed.): Pension Design and Structure: New Lessons from Behavioral Finance. Oxford University Press, 83-95.

Jensen, Michael C., and William H. Meckling. 1976. "Theory of the Firm: Managerial Behavior, Agency Costs, and Ownership Structure." *Journal of Financial Economics* 3(4): 78-79.

Loewenstein, George, Daylian M. Cain, and Sunita Sah. 2011. "The Limits of Transparency: Pitfalls and Potential of Disclosing Conflicts of Interest." *The American Economic Review* 101(3): 423-428.

Lusardi, Annamaria, and Olivia S. Mitchell. 2007. "Financial Literacy and Retirement Preparedness: Evidence and Implications for Financial Education Programs." *Michigan Retirement Research Center Research Working Paper* 2006-144.

Lusardi, Annamaria, Olivia S. Mitchell, and Vilsa Curto. 2009. "Financial Literacy and Financial Sophistication among Older Americans." *National Bureau of Economic Research Working Paper* 15469.

Malmendier, Ulrike, and Devin Shanthikumar. 2007. "Are Small Investors Naive About Incentives?." *Journal of Financial Economics* 85 (2): 457-489.

Mullainathan, Sendhil, Markus Noeth, and Antoinette Schoar. 2012. "The Market for Financial Advice: An Audit Study." National Bureau of Economic Research Working Paper 17929.

Prentice, Robert A. 2011. "Moral Equilibrium: Stock Brokers and the Limits of Disclosure." Wisconsin Law Review: 1059.

Securities and Exchange Commission (SEC). 2007. "Protecting Senior Investors: Report of Examinations of Securities Firms Providing `Free Lunch' Sales Seminar." http://www.sec.gov/spotlight/seniors/ freelunchr eport.pdf.

—. 2011. "Study on Investment Advisers and Broker-Dealers." http://www.sec.gov/news/studies/2011/913studyfinal.pdf.

Turner, John A. and Dana M. Muir. 2013. "The Market for Financial Advisers." In Olivia S. Mitchell and Kent Smetters (Ed.): The Market for Retirement Financial Advice. Oxford University Press, 13- 45.

Vanguard. 2014. "How America Saves 2014: A Report on Vanguard 2013 Defined Contribution Plan Data." https://pressroom.vanguard.com/content/nonindexed/How_America_Saves_2014.pdf.

End Notes

[1] This report uses the term defined contribution plan to refer to employer-based defined contribution retirement plans (i.e. excluding IRAs).

[2] In Figure 1, the annuities category excludes annuities held by IRAs, 403(b) plans, 457 plans, and private pension funds.

[3] For simplicity, this report refers to both firms and the individual advisers working at those firms as brokers and RIAs.

[4] See Financial Industry Regulatory Authority (FINRA) (2013), Howat and Reid (2007), Hung et al. (2008), Turner and Muir (2013), and Prentice (2011) for additional discussion of conflicts. 5 Conflicted payments are often split between the adviser and the adviser's firm. The allocation between the two affects the size of the financial incentive the payments create, but not generally the nature of the incentive created.

[6] According to the Survey of Consumer Finances, nearly half of American families held retirement savings accounts, including DC plans and IRAs, in 2013. Outside of retirement accounts and pension plans, only 14 percent held individual stocks, only 8 percent held mutual funds or other pooled investment funds, and even fewer held CDs, individual bonds, or other managed assets.

[7] Variable annuity mutual fund assets are classified with mutual funds, not annuities.

[8] The authors find outperformance of foreign equity funds, but this result is attributable to a small number of large funds sold through a single fund family.

[9] While the authors do not find a statistically significant effect of unusually high or low revenue-sharing payments on performance, their point estimate is negative, consistent with—though not dispositive of—reduced performance resulting from unusually high revenue-sharing payments as well.

[10] The dollar value of load funds and non-institutional mutual fund assets in 2013 is from Investment Company Institute (ICI) (2014). The total value of mutual fund assets in IRAs at the end of 2013 is from ICI's "The U.S. Retirement Market, Third Quarter 2014" available at http://www.ici.org/research/stats/retirement.

[11] The share of IRA owners relying on professional retirement advice is from Holden and Schrass (2015).

[12] See Engel and McCoy (2002) for a discussion of loan markets; for a focus on elderly individuals in financial markets, see Infogroup/ORC (2010) and SEC (2007).

[13] See, for example, Barber and Odean (2000, 2001, 2002, 2013), Benartzi and Thaler (2001), Choi et al. (2011), Calvet et al. (2007).

In: Retirement Savings ...
Editor: Florence P. Marsh

ISBN: 978-1-63482-724-9

Chapter 3

401(K) PLANS: IMPROVED REGULATION COULD BETTER PROTECT PARTICIPANTS FROM CONFLICTS OF INTEREST*

United States Government Accountability Office

WHY GAO DID THIS STUDY

Recent volatility in financial markets highlights the need for prudent investment decisions if 401(k) plans are to provide an adequate source of retirement income. While plan sponsors and participants may receive help in assessing their investment choices, concerns have been raised about the impartiality of the advice provided. GAO was asked to describe circumstances where service providers may have conflicts of interest in providing assistance related to the selection of investment options for (1) plan sponsors and (2) plan participants, and (3) steps the Department of Labor (Labor) has taken to address conflicts of interest related to the selection of investment options.

* This is an edited, reformatted and augmented version of a U.S. Government Accountability Office report, GAO-11-119, issued January 2011.

What GAO Recommends

GAO recommends that Labor amend pending regulations to require that service providers disclose compensation and fiduciary status in a consistent, summary format and revise current standards, which permit a service provider to highlight investment options in which it has a financial interest. GAO also recommends that the Department of the Treasury amend proposed regulations to require disclosure that investment products outside a plan typically have higher fees than products available within a plan. Overall, Labor and Treasury generally agreed to consider our recommendations as they evaluate comments received on pending regulations.

What GAO Found

The sponsors of 401(k) plans face conflicts of interest from service providers assisting in the selection of investment options because of third-party payments and other business arrangements. For example, providers who help sponsors to establish and maintain their plans may receive third-party payments from investment fund companies. The payments, sometimes called revenue sharing, create a conflict of interest because the provider may receive greater compensation from certain funds. Moreover, providers are reported to commonly structure their relationships with sponsors in a manner that avoids being subject to fiduciary standards under the Employee Retirement Income Security Act (ERISA). According to several industry experts, many sponsors, particularly of smaller plans, do not understand whether or not providers to the plan are fiduciaries, nor are they aware that the provider's compensation may vary based on the investment options selected. Such conflicts could lead to higher costs for the plan, which are typically borne by participants.

In certain situations, participants face conflicts of interest from providers that have a financial interest when providing investment assistance. For example, although investment education is defined as generalized investment information, providers may highlight their own funds as examples of investments available within asset classes even though they may have a financial interest in the funds. According to industry experts, participants perceive education as investment advice. Thus, participants may not understand that the provider is not a fiduciary adviser required to act solely in participants' best interests. Also, several industry experts expressed concerns that providers stand to gain higher profits from marketing investment products outside of plans to participants, a practice known as cross-selling. For example, if participants use their plan provider for Individual Retirement Account rollovers, they may not understand, because of insufficient disclosures, that fees are often higher for products offered outside the plan and that the provider may not be serving as a fiduciary adviser. Consequently, participants may choose funds that do not meet their needs and pay higher fees, which reduce their retirement savings.

While Labor has taken steps to address the potential for conflicted investment advice provided to sponsors and participants, more can be done to ensure they receive impartial advice. In fiscal year 2007, the Employee Benefits Security Administration (EBSA) began a national enforcement project that focuses on the receipt of improper or undisclosed compensation by certain providers, but its enforcement efforts are constrained to fiduciary providers and limited by EBSA's approach for generating cases. In addition, EBSA issued regulations to revise the definition of an ERISA fiduciary and require enhanced disclosure of providers' compensation and fiduciary status. These regulations, as currently specified, would help EBSA and sponsors detect and deter conflicted investment advice. However, the regulations do not require that certain disclosures be made in consistent or summary formats, which may leave sponsors with information that is not sufficient or comparable.

ABBREVIATIONS

bps	basis points
CAP	Consultant/Adviser Project
DB	defined benefit
DC	defined contribution
EBSA	Employee Benefits Security Administration
EIAA	eligible investment advice arrangement
ERISA	Employee Retirement Income Security Act
FINRA	Financial Industry Regulatory Authority, Inc.
ICI	Investment Company Institute
IRA	individual retirement account
IRS	Internal Revenue Service
NASD	National Association of Securities Dealers
OIG	Office of Inspector General

PPA	Pension Protection Act
PSCA	Profit Sharing/401(k) Council of America
QDIA	qualified default investment alternative
RIA	registered investment advisor
SEC	Securities and Exchange Commission
SHRM	Society for Human Resource Management
SIPP	Survey of Income and Program Participation
SPARK	Society of Professional Asset-Managers and Record Keepers
SRO	self-regulatory organization

* * *

January 28, 2011

The Honorable George Miller
Ranking Member
House Education and the Workforce Committee
United States House of Representatives

Dear Mr. Miller:

In recent high-profile court cases, 401(k) plan participants allege they have lost millions of dollars because of investment options that benefited the plan's service provider at the expense of participants.[1] Plan sponsors and participants may rely on investment education or advice from their service provider to help them assess their investment choices at two key points: first, when the plan sponsor decides which investment options to include in the plan, and second, when each plan participant decides where to invest his or her assets given the available options in the plan. However, questions have been raised about the impartiality of the assistance provided when the service provider has a conflict of interest. A conflict of interest occurs when someone in a position of trust, like a pension plan adviser, has competing professional or personal financial interests. For example, the structure of advisers' compensation and their other business arrangements could create competing interests that may bias their investment recommendations to plan sponsors or participants. If left unchecked, conflicts of interest could lead plan sponsors or participants to select investment options with higher fees or mediocre performance, which, while beneficial to the service provider, could amount to a significant reduction in retirement savings over a worker's career.

The potential for financial harm to participants from conflicted investment advice has raised questions about its nature and extent in 401(k) plans. To better understand how conflicts of interest may arise in investment assistance provided to plan sponsors or participants and to evaluate how such conflicts are addressed by current and proposed regulations, you asked us to address the following questions:

1. What are circumstances where service providers may have conflicts of interest in providing assistance related to the selection of investment options by plan sponsors?
2. What are circumstances where service providers may have conflicts of interest in providing assistance related to the selection of investment options by plan participants?
3. What steps has the Department of Labor (Labor) taken to address conflicts of interest related to the selection of investment options?

To answer these questions, we reviewed relevant research and federal laws and regulations on investment advice arrangements for plan sponsors and participants. We conducted interviews with 401(k) plan service providers, government officials, and other industry experts to identify different practices that may create conflicts of interest in the provision of investment advice to plan sponsors and participants. In addition, we reviewed relevant Securities and Exchange Commission (SEC) and Labor enforcement cases and spoke with field investigators to examine revenue-sharing arrangements and other business practices where conflicts of interest were identified. To identify current practices in participant-level investment advice, we conducted a poll of plan sponsors and service providers in partnership with the Society for Human Resource Management (SHRM) and the Society of Professional Asset-Managers and Record Keepers (SPARK). In addition, we obtained and analyzed data from service providers, the Investment Company Institute (ICI), and the Survey of Income and Program Participation (SIPP) to ascertain the percentage of plan participants who have transferred or rolled 401(k) plan assets into individual retirement accounts (IRA). We assessed the reliability of the data we present and found the data to be sufficiently reliable as used in this report. To determine the extent to which Labor's actions address the potential for conflicted investment advice, we reviewed relevant federal laws and regulations and interviewed Labor's Employee Benefits Security

Administration (EBSA) officials, including Consultant/Adviser Project and field investigators, and industry experts. In addition, we reviewed reports and interviewed officials from Labor's Office of Inspector General (OIG) who evaluated EBSA's efforts to protect pension plan assets from conflicts of interest in pension plan service providers. We also interviewed service providers and industry experts on the likely impact of recent regulations issued by Labor pertaining to investment advice to participants and disclosure of compensation received by service providers. For additional information on the methodology used in this review, see appendix I.

We conducted this performance audit from January 2010 through January 2011 in accordance with generally accepted government auditing standards. Those standards require that we plan and perform the audit to obtain sufficient, appropriate evidence to provide a reasonable basis for our findings and conclusions based on our audit objectives. We believe that the evidence obtained provides a reasonable basis for our findings and conclusions based on our audit objectives.

Background

In contrast to workers in a traditional defined benefit (DB) plan, workers in a 401(k) plan, the predominant type of defined contribution (DC) plan in the United States, have more control over their retirement assets, but also bear greater responsibility and risk in the investment of assets. In a typical 401(k) plan, workers decide whether or not to make contributions into an individual account. Contributions may also be made by their employer. Participants direct these contributions to mutual funds and other financial market investments to accumulate pension benefits, dependent on investment returns net of fees. As we reported in 2006, investment fees are usually paid by participants and administrative fees are often paid by employers, but participants bear them in a growing number of plans.[2] Depending on contributions and net investment returns, participants accumulate an account balance that will then be withdrawn at or after retirement. Over the last decade, participation in DC plans among all private industry employees has increased from 36 percent in 1999 to 43 percent in 2008.[3] In 2008, about 49.8 million workers actively participated in a 401(k) plan.[4]

The degree of responsibility and risk borne by workers in 401(k) plans underscores the need for prudent investment decisions if these plans are to provide an adequate source of income in retirement. Poor investment decisions—either by the plan sponsors when they decide which investment options to offer in the plans, or by participants when, given these options, they decide where to invest their assets—can result in lower returns and correspondingly less retirement savings. Several studies have found that, from 1988 to 2006, DC plans underperformed DB plans by 1 percentage point or more, which may be explained by higher fees in 401(k) plans and a lack of diversification in participants' investment allocations.[5] Numerous studies on financial literacy have also pointed to the need to educate participants to improve their investment decision-making and savings outcomes.[6] For example, one study found that a large percentage of American workers have not conducted meaningful retirement planning, even when retirement is in the near future.[7] Another study found that most workers acknowledge they do not know as much as they should about retirement planning and that many workers actually guessed at their retirement savings needs.[8]

To address the challenges of investment risk in 401(k) plans, both plan sponsors and participants may seek assistance from service providers in selecting investment options. At the plan sponsor level, many plans rely heavily on the expertise and guidance of their advisers when making investment decisions. The service providers that offer these advisory services to plan sponsors can vary considerably in their business arrangements. While some service providers operate as independent, "fee-only" advisers, who are compensated solely by their clients and do not receive additional compensation contingent on the purchase or sale of a financial product, other service providers offer affiliated services, including brokerage and money management, in addition to advisory services. As shown in figure 1, service providers can be used to provide a number of services necessary to operate a 401(k) plan, which can be bundled or unbundled with investment management services or advisory services. Under a bundled service arrangement, the plan sponsor hires a company that provides multiple services directly or through subcontracts.

At the participant level, advisory services can also be provided through a variety of methods, including call centers or help desks, group seminars, one-on-one sessions, computer models (e.g., software that estimates future retirement income needs or asset allocation models), or brochures and other printed materials provided by plan service providers. When providing this assistance to participants, a service provider may furnish either investment education or investment advice. As specified by EBSA, investment education consists of general investment information, including general information about the plan and asset allocation models that is not tailored to the needs or interests of an individual plan participant (see table 1).[9] Investment advice, on the other hand, consists of one or more individualized investment recommendations tailored to a participant's particular investment needs.

While plan sponsors and participants may rely on service providers for assistance in making investment decisions, concerns have been raised about the independence of the advice provided in some cases. A 2005 SEC report noted that its examination of investment advisers providing pension consultant services found that many such consultants provide services to both plans and money managers, a situation that has the potential to compromise the objectivity of the consultant's recommendations to the plan.[10] Namely, the report states that concerns exist that consultants may steer plans to hire certain money managers or other vendors based on the consultant's (or an affiliate's) other business relationships and receipt of fees from these firms, rather than because the money manager is best suited to the plan's needs. As we reported in 2007, no complete information exists about the presence of conflicts of interest at pension plan service providers.[11] However, the 2005 SEC examination of the activities of 24 pension consultants from 2002 through 2003 revealed that 13 out of 24 of the service providers examined failed to disclose significant ongoing conflicts of interest, such as affiliated businesses or compensation received from money managers.[12]

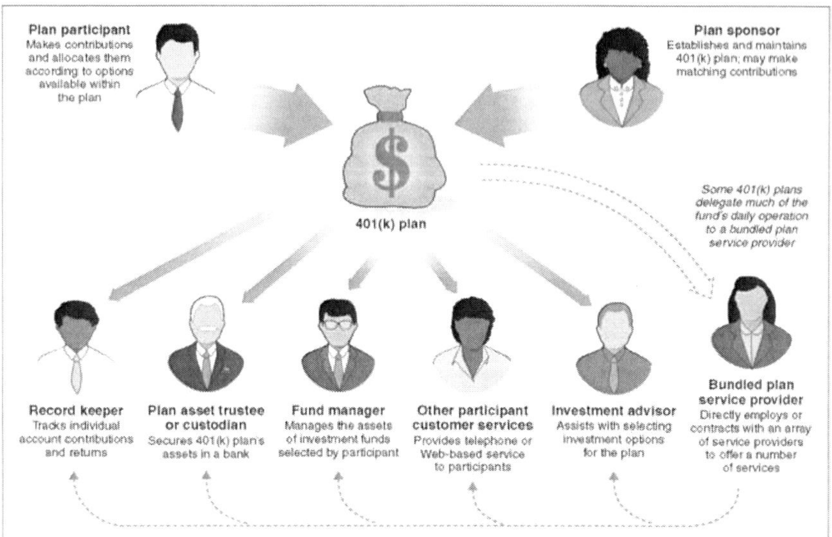

Source: GAO analysis of information from industry practitioners.

Figure 1. Structure of Service Provider Arrangements in 401(k) Plans.

Table 1. EBSA's Definition of Investment Education

In June 1996, EBSA issued an interpretive bulletin defining participant investment education (codified at 29 C.F.R. § 2509.96-1(d)). The bulletin identified specific categories of investment-related information that, when furnished to plan participants or beneficiaries, would not constitute the rendering of investment advice under the Employee Retirement Income Security Act of 1974 (ERISA). The categories of information include the following:
• **Plan information**—information and materials that inform a participant or beneficiary about the benefits of plan participation, the impact of preretirement withdrawals on retirement income, the terms and operation of the plan, and other general plan information. Such information cannot reference the appropriateness of any investment option for a particular participant or beneficiary.
• **General financial and investment information**—information and materials that inform a participant or beneficiary about, among other things, general financial and investment concepts, historic differences in rates of return between different asset classes, effects of inflation, and estimating future retirement income needs. Such general information cannot directly relate to any investment alternatives available to participants and beneficiaries.
• **Asset allocation models**—information and materials that provide a participant or beneficiary with models of asset allocation portfolios of hypothetical individuals with different time horizons and risk profiles. If an asset allocation model identifies specific investment alternatives available under a plan, the model must be accompanied by a statement that other investment alternatives having similar risk and return characteristics may be available under the plan.
• **Interactive investment materials**—includes questionnaires, worksheets, software, and similar materials that provide a participant or beneficiary the means to estimate future retirement income needs and assess the impact of different asset allocations on retirement income.

Source: GAO review of EBSA's interpretive bulletin relating to participant investment education (codified at 29 C.F.R. § 2509.96-1(d)).

Regulation of Investment Advice

ERISA

Investment advice provided to plan sponsors and participants and any related conflicts of interest are regulated under ERISA. ERISA states that a person who renders investment advice for a fee or other compensation, direct or indirect, with respect to any moneys or property of a plan or has any authority or responsibility to do so is a fiduciary and thus is subject to fiduciary standards outlined in the law and regulations.[13] This statutory definition of fiduciary for investment advice is currently subject to a five-part test, set forth in regulations, each element of which must be met for an individual to be considered a fiduciary.[14] Specifically, under this test, a consultant or adviser is determined to be providing investment advice only if the advice was provided for a fee either direct or indirect, and the advice was provided

1. as to the value of securities or other property or as to the advisability of investing in, purchasing, or selling securities or other property;
2. on a regular basis;
3. pursuant to a mutual agreement, arrangement, or understanding;
4. as a primary basis for investment decisions; and
5. based on the particular needs of the plan.[15]

Although plan sponsors often rely on consultants and other service providers to assist them in asset management, which includes selecting money managers and monitoring money managers' performance and brokerage transactions, not all of these consultants and service providers are at all times fiduciaries under ERISA based on the application of the five-part test.

For plan sponsors and other service providers who are fiduciaries, ERISA requires they discharge duties solely in the interest of the participants and beneficiaries with care, skill, prudence, and diligence.[16] Although ERISA generally prohibits fiduciaries from acting on conflicts of interest, certain transactions are strictly precluded under prohibited transaction rules, regardless of whether or not participants are harmed.[17] In particular, prohibited transaction rules preclude fiduciaries from "self-dealing," which includes an individual dealing with plan assets for his or her own benefit.[18] In addition, EBSA has explained that ERISA obligates fiduciaries to obtain and consider information relating to the cost of plan services and potential conflicts of interest presented by such service arrangements.[19]

EBSA is responsible for enforcing these provisions of Title I of ERISA, as well as educating and assisting plan participants, beneficiaries, and plan sponsors. Fiduciaries that breach their plan duties are personally liable for making up losses to the plan and restoring any profits made through the use of plan assets. In addition, they may face removal as plan fiduciaries.[20] Participants may also seek recovery against nonfiduciaries in certain circumstances.[21] In addition to carrying out its enforcement responsibilities, EBSA assists regulated parties in complying with ERISA by issuing technical guidance, including advisory opinions and interpretive bulletins, and educating plan participants, beneficiaries, and plan sponsors.

Securities Laws

In addition to being regulated by ERISA, investment advice and conflicts of interest are also regulated under securities laws. SEC regulates certain money managers and pension consultants under the Investment Advisers Act of 1940 (Advisers Act), which requires those firms meeting certain criteria to register with the commission as investment advisers.[22] For these registered investment advisers, SEC requires that they disclose information about affiliations, business interests, and compensation arrangements to their advisory clients, primarily by providing a brochure that meets the requirements of Part 2 of SEC's Form ADV to new and prospective clients. In addition, registered investment advisers must annually deliver either an updated brochure with a summary of material changes or a summary of material changes and offer to provide an updated copy of the brochure.[23] According to SEC, all investment advisers—whether registered with SEC or not—have a fiduciary obligation under the Advisers Act to avoid conflicts of interest and, at a minimum, make full disclosure of material conflicts of interest to their clients. When an adviser fails to disclose information regarding material conflicts of interest, clients are unable to make informed decisions about entering into or continuing the advisory relationship. Failure to act in accordance with requirements under the Advisers Act may constitute a violation. If SEC becomes aware of conflicts of interest that are inadequately disclosed or pose harm to investors, it can take enforcement action against the service provider. SEC also regulates broker-dealers under the Securities Exchange Act of 1934 (Exchange Act), which requires that broker-dealers register with SEC, unless an exception or exemption applies. In addition, broker-dealers that deal with the public must become members of the Financial Industry Regulatory Authority, Inc. (FINRA).[24] Under the anti-fraud provisions of the federal securities laws, including just and equitable principles of trade, broker-dealers are required to deal fairly with their customers. Salespersons of broker-dealers are subject to licensing requirements, including examinations. Broker-dealers are held to a suitability standard when rendering investment recommendations.[25] When a broker-dealer makes a recommendation to buy, exchange, or sell a security to a retail investor, that broker-dealer must recommend only those securities that the broker reasonably believes are suitable for the customer. In addition, a broker-dealer must disclose all material information regarding the security and the recommendation,[26] including, among other things, any material adverse facts or material conflicts of interest.[27] However, according to FINRA staff, up-front general disclosure of a broker-dealer's business activities and relationships that may cause conflicts of interest with retail customers is not required.[28] SEC staff has noted that, in practice, with broker-dealers, required disclosures of conflicts have been more limited than with investment advisers and apply at different points in the relationship.[29] Table 2 provides a comparison of the standards of conduct required by ERISA, and those required of investment advisers and broker-dealers.

Recent Legislation

The Dodd-Frank Wall Street Reform and Consumer Protection Act (Dodd-Frank), signed into law on July 21, 2010, includes provisions that amend the Advisers Act and the Exchange Act that affect investment advisers and broker-dealers. Under these provisions, SEC, among other things, conducted a 6-month study on the effectiveness of existing standards of care for broker-dealers and investment advisers and examined whether there are legal and regulatory gaps, shortcomings, or overlaps in legal or regulatory standards in the protection of retail customers.[30] Based on its review, SEC staff recommended that SEC propose rules that apply a uniform standard of conduct which requires broker-dealers and investment advisers, when providing personalized investment advice to retail customers, to act in the best interest of the customer without regard to the financial or other interest of the broker, dealer, or investment adviser. SEC staff also recommended that SEC should facilitate the provision of uniform, simple and clear disclosures to retail customers about the terms of their relationships with broker-dealers and investment advisers, including any material conflicts of interest.[31]

SERVICE PROVIDERS MAY HAVE CONFLICTS OF INTEREST IN PROVIDING INVESTMENT ASSISTANCE TO PLAN SPONSORS BECAUSE OF THIRD-PARTY PAYMENTS AND OTHER BUSINESS ARRANGEMENTS

Service Providers' Business Arrangements May Create Conflicts of Interest in Investment Assistance Provided to Plan Sponsors

Several industry experts we spoke with cited third-party payments, also known as revenue sharing, as a potential conflict of interest for service providers involved in the fund selection process for a 401(k) plan. Revenue sharing, in the pension plan industry, generally refers to indirect payments made from one service provider, such as the investment fund provider, to another service provider in connection with services provided to the plan, rather than payments made directly by the plan sponsor for plan services.[32] According to industry experts, revenue sharing is a widespread practice among 401(k) service providers. As we have previously reported, revenue-sharing payments can be used to offset expenses the plan has agreed to pay and thus be cost-neutral to the plan.[33] However, as shown in figure 2, revenue sharing may, depending on the circumstances, also create a conflict of interest if it is not structured to be cost-neutral to the plan and may result in increased compensation to service providers. Industry experts we spoke with explained that this situation creates an incentive for the service provider to suggest funds with higher revenue-sharing payments. Because of these conflicts of interest, the service provider may suggest funds that have poorer performance or higher costs for participants compared with other available funds. The amount of revenue-sharing payments can vary considerably, both across investment funds and within a fund through different share classes.[34] Documentation we obtained showed revenue-sharing payments from hundreds of share classes of different investment funds that ranged from 5 to 125 basis points (bps). Given this variation, EBSA field investigators told us that a service provider might only recommend or include fund share classes that pay higher revenue sharing and exclude other fund share classes that pay lower or no revenue sharing.

As described in table 3, revenue sharing can include various forms of payments, such as 12b-1 fees, that may create conflicts of interest for service providers assisting with the selection of investment options for a 401(k) plan.

Besides creating a potential conflict of interest, using revenue sharing to reimburse for record-keeping expenses can have other adverse effects on the plan and participants. Service providers told us these payments are often not clearly disclosed to the plan. As shown in figure 3, this could result in participants paying a greater or lesser share of record-keeping expenses depending on which funds they choose to invest their assets. Further, because subtransfer agent fees are based on the amount of assets under management, the record-keeping costs increase as the fund grows and may get quite large if not revised. According to one service provider we interviewed, these fees can result in the plan continuing to pay more for record-keeping services as assets grow, although the cost of providing record-keeping services tends to remain the same.

Table 2. Basic Summary of Standards of Conduct for Investment Service Providers under Federal Law

Applicable federal law	Standard of conduct	Who must abide by standard of conduct	Specific requirements and prohibitions
Employee Retirement Income Security Act of 1974	*ERISA fiduciary standard (prudent man standard of care)*:[a] Fiduciary must render services solely in the best interest of plan participants and beneficiaries.	*ERISA fiduciary*: A person who renders investment advice for a fee or other compensation. Additionally, a person is a fiduciary with respect to a plan to the extent (1) he exercises any discretionary authority or control respecting management of such plan and plan assets, and (2) he has any discretionary authority or responsibility in the administration of such plan. See 29 U.S.C. § 1002(21) for a more detailed description of this provision.	Requires that fiduciaries with respect to the plan not engage in prohibited transactions, as specified in the statute.[b] As such, a conflict of interest does not represent a violation of ERISA's prohibited transaction rules unless, based on the facts and circumstances, it constitutes self-dealing. EBSA notes that ERISA §404(a) continues to obligate fiduciaries to obtain and consider information relating to potential conflicts of interest by such service arrangements.[c]
The Investment Advisers Act of 1940	*Advisers Act fiduciary standard*:[d] Person has an affirmative duty to render services solely in the best interests of clients.	*Investment adviser*: Person who, for compensation, is engaged in the business of advising others as to the value of securities or the purchase or sale of securities.	Requires advisers to eliminate or disclose material conflicts of interest to clients.[e]
Securities Exchange Act of 1934 and rules	*Regulatory requirements*:[f] Broker-dealers are required to deal fairly with customers. Specific obligations are imposed	*Brokers or dealers*: *Brokers*: Person engaged in the business of effecting transactions in securities for the account of others.	Requires brokers to comply with rules governing their conduct, including the suitability standard, as well as to disclose material conflicts

Applicable federal law	Standard of conduct	Who must abide by standard of conduct	Specific requirements and prohibitions
from SEC and self-regulatory organizations	regarding suitability, fair pricing, communications with customers, disclosure, and other business conduct obligations.[g]	*Dealers*: Person engaged in the business of buying and selling securities.	of interest when making recommendations to customers.

Source: GAO analysis of ERISA and securities laws and regulations.

[a] ERISA requires a fiduciary to render services in accordance with a prudent man standard of care, with the care, skill, prudence, and diligence that a prudent man acting in a like capacity and familiar with such matter would use in the conduct. See 29 U.S.C. §1104(a)(1) for a more detailed description of this provision.

[b] See 29 U.S.C. § 1106 for more information about ERISA's prohibited transactions rules.

[c] 45 Fed. Reg. 41,603 (Preamble to the Interim Final 408(b)(2) regulations) (July 16, 2010).

[d] In SEC v. Capital Gains Research Bureau, 375 U.S. 180 (1963), the Supreme Court recognized that the Advisers Act imposes a fiduciary duty on investment advisers. This standard imposes an affirmative duty to act solely in the best interests of the client. The investment adviser must eliminate or disclose all conflicts of interest.

[e] SEC has, in effect, established rules of conduct for investment advisers, including requirements for disclosing of conflicts of interest, obtaining the best execution on behalf of clients, allocating investments among clients fairly, ensuring that investments are suitable for clients, and ensuring that there is a reasonable basis for recommendations. SEC also requires investment advisers to maintain records pertaining to client accounts and business operations.

[f] The standards of conduct for broker-dealers are also based on antifraud provisions of the securities law and agency principles. Broker-dealers also have a duty of fairness in their contracts with customers and specific business conduct obligations under SRO rules. Broker-dealers that handle discretionary accounts or that have a relationship of trust and confidence are generally thought to owe fiduciary obligations to their customers.

[g] Duties imposed on broker-dealers by the Exchange Act include the duty to supervise persons subject to supervision and the duty to keep records and file reports.

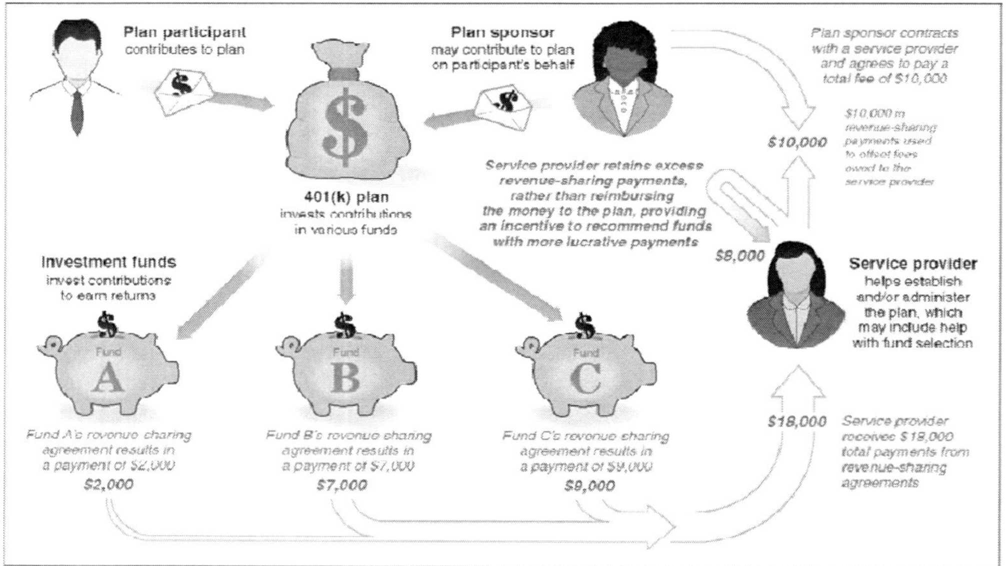

Source: GAO analysis of information from industry practitioners.

Note: In the example above, the service provider receives revenue-sharing payments from three funds offered by the 401(k) plan, which amount to $18,000. The service provider is owed $10,000 in fees for assistance provided to the plan. Of the $18,000 received in revenue-sharing payments, $10,000 is used to offset the fees owed to the service provider. The service provider has a conflict of interest because, rather than reimbursing the remaining $8,000 to the plan, the service provider retains the remainder as revenue.

Figure 2. Revenue-Sharing Arrangement That Entails a Conflict of Interest for the Service Provider.

Table 3. Examples of Potential Conflicts of Interest for Service Providers from Revenue Sharing and Other Third-Party Payments

Source of potential conflict	Explanation of payments	Potential conflict of interest
12b-1 fees	Fees known as 12b-1 fees, which EBSA field investigators told us can range from 25 to 100 bps, are paid out of fund assets to other service providers for several purposes, including the following: • paying sales-based compensation, • covering marketing expenses,[a] or • for shareholder services.[b]	A service provider may increase its compensation by not refunding or only partially refunding 12b-1 fees to the plan. In some cases, EBSA officials and an industry expert told us that if a fund stops paying 12b-1 fees to a service provider, the service provider may recommend changes to plans to replace funds that no longer pay 12b-1 fees with other funds that pay these fees.
Other sales-based payments, such as front-end or deferred sales loads	A front-end or deferred sales load is charged to investors as a percentage of their investment, generally when they initially invest or redeem their shares, and is used to compensate another party for selling fund shares.[c] EBSA field investigators and a service provider representative said that some service providers receive payments of about 100 bps in addition to 12b-1 fees.	If a service provider can increase its compensation through payments from investment funds, it creates a conflict of interest. The service provider has the incentive to recommend funds with higher sales loads or other payments over funds that have lower or no such payments. Example: • In a 2006 EBSA enforcement case, a service provider was found to have steered pension plan clients, including 401(k) plans, to invest in a hedge fund that, in turn, paid the service provider an incentive fee. The service provider did not disclose the incentive fee arrangement it had with the hedge fund to its pension plan clients, although it was required to do so. This case is still in litigation.
Subtransfer agent fees	Subtransfer agent fees are used to reimburse a plan's record keeper for shareholder services the fund would have otherwise provided, such as maintaining participant-level accounts and distributing the fund's prospectus. EBSA field investigators told us that some	According to an industry expert, the payment of subtransfer agent fees is a potential conflict of interest because a service provider may receive most of its compensation from a few funds, so it has the incentive to recommend that those funds be kept in the plan even if they offer inferior performance.[d]

Table 3. (Continued)

Source of potential conflict	Explanation of payments	Potential conflict of interest
	funds do not pay any subtransfer agent fees, while others pay between 10 and 20 bps. A representative from a large bundled service provider told us the fees received for record-keeping reimbursements from outside funds can range from zero to 40 bps.	Representatives from an advisory firm to many large plans said that, in some cases, a service provider will only recommend funds that pay subtransfer agent fees or other fees back to the provider, which may use these fees to cover expenses or for extra revenue without disclosing this arrangement to plan sponsors or participants.

Source: GAO analysis based on information from industry practitioners and EBSA enforcement cases.

Note: A conflict of interest may or may not be a violation of ERISA or applicable securities laws, depending on the facts and circumstances.

[a] Under FINRA rules, 12b-1 fees that are used to pay marketing and distribution expenses (as opposed to shareholder service expenses) cannot exceed 75 bps of a fund's average net assets per year. NASD Conduct Rule 2830(d)(2)(E).

[b] SEC Rule 12b-1 allows mutual funds to pay for marketing and distribution expenses directly from fund assets. Not all funds pay 12b-1 fees and, within a fund, some share classes may pay 12b-1 fees while other share classes do not. While 12b-1 fees are included in a fund's expense ratio, SEC has noted that many investors do not understand these fees nor are they aware the fees are being deducted from their investments. SEC has proposed new rules to replace Rule 12b-1 with a new framework that would separately regulate service fees and asset-based sales charges. See Mutual Fund Distribution Fees; Confirmations, 75 Fed. Reg. 47,064 (August 4, 2010).

[c] SEC does not limit the size of sales load a fund may charge, but FINRA does not permit mutual fund sales loads to exceed 8.5 percent. The percentage is lower if a fund imposes other types of charges. NASD Conduct Rule 2830(d)(1)(2). Both 12b-1fees and sales loads are required to be disclosed in a fund's prospectus and annual report. A payment to sales personnel can be made through onetime charges against fund assets or it can be built into ongoing fees for the fund.

[d] A record keeper may function as a bundled service provider and also provide investment assistance.

Payments from Brokerage Firms to Other Service Providers

In addition to revenue-sharing payments from fund companies, payments from brokerage firms, which execute trades for participants' investment funds, to other service providers can also create conflicts of interest related to a 401(k) plan's investments. For example, in a 2007 SEC case, an investment adviser was alleged to have advised its pension plan clients, including 401(k) plans, to use a specific brokerage firm under certain circumstances. The brokerage firm allegedly paid the service provider annual compensation based in part on the amount of commissions generated, which the adviser failed to disclose to its pension plan clients although the adviser was required to do so.[35] The contingent compensation from the brokerage firm to the investment adviser created an incentive for the service provider to steer plans to use that particular brokerage firm.

In other cases, industry experts told us that, at the request of an investment adviser, brokerage firms can use commission revenues from trading shares to make payments to other service providers that can create conflicts of interests if not handled properly. Under the Securities Exchange Act of 1934, investment advisers are permitted to pay broker-dealers more than the lowest available commission rate for trading shares under certain circumstances.[36] The investment adviser can direct the broker-dealer to use the commission revenues to pay the fees of other service providers or to purchase services of value to investors, such as investment research to improve the management of the fund.[37] However, if the commission revenues are not used for the benefit of the plan, it could create a conflict of interest. A 2005 SEC report concerning examinations of pension consultants identifies several areas of concern and examples of poorly managed conflicts of interest.[38] For example,

- Using commission revenues to pay for another service provider's fees, (i.e., a "commission recapture" arrangement) such as for a pension consultant, can result in greater compensation to that service provider, because such arrangements may not be capped to terminate when fees due to the service provider have been paid in full, resulting in the plan overpaying for services.
- These arrangements are not always well documented and raise concerns that plans may not receive "best execution," meaning that the plan's service provider may recommend that the plan use a broker-dealer with whom it has such an arrangement even if the broker-dealer does not offer the most favorable terms for the plan.
- These arrangements can also create the incentive for the service provider to recommend a more active trading strategy to increase the number of transactions and, consequently, the amount of commissions.

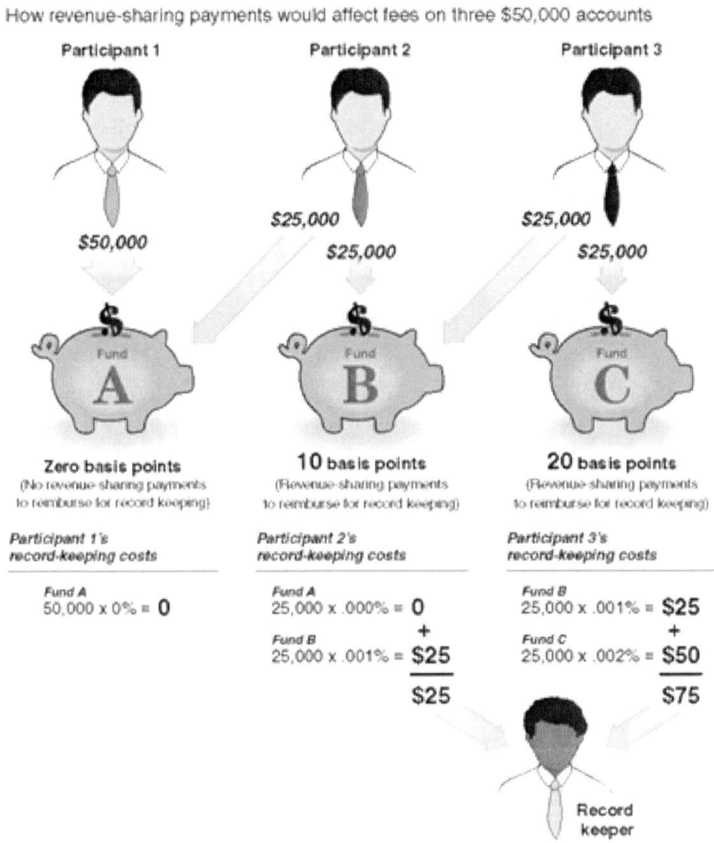

Source: GAO analysis of information from industry practitioners.

Note: In the example above, each participant has an account balance of $50,000 that he allocates to different investment options in his 401(k) plan. Record-keeping expenses for the plan are paid through revenue-sharing payments from funds B and C. Because participant 1 invests exclusively in fund A, which does not have any revenue-sharing payments, he does not pay any record-keeping fees. Participant 2 invests half of his account balance in fund A, which has no revenue-sharing payments, and half in fund B, which has revenue-sharing payments. Thus, participant 2 pays some record-keeping fees through his investments in fund B. Participant 3 pays the most in record-keeping fees because he invests exclusively in funds that make revenue-sharing payments.

Figure 3. Potential Impact of Revenue Sharing on Distribution of Record-Keeping Costs among Participants with Equivalent Account Balances.

Other Business Arrangements That May Create Conflicts of Interest

In addition to payments among service providers, other types of business arrangements can also create conflicts of interest. As shown in table 4, service providers may have affiliated businesses, such as proprietary investment funds or a brokerage arm, that can profit from the investment of plan assets. For example, a service provider that offers its own investment funds has the incentive to steer plan sponsors to select these proprietary funds even if other funds are available from different providers that better suit the needs of the plan.

Table 4. Examples of Potential Conflicts of Interest from a Service Provider's Affiliated Businesses

Source of potential conflict from affiliated businesses	Potential conflict of interest
Bundled service provider with proprietary investment funds	A service provider has an incentive to recommend its own funds to the plan even if other funds that better suit the needs of the plan might be available from other fund providers. Industry experts we interviewed gave the following examples: • Bundled providers may require plan sponsors to include their proprietary funds as investment options in the plan as a prerequisite to servicing the plan.
	• Bundled providers may require the plan to designate one of their proprietary funds as the qualified default investment alternative (QDIA).[a] Representatives of bundled service providers that offer proprietary funds we spoke with said that they do not offer investment advice as ERISA fiduciaries. However, representatives from other service providers told us that many plans rely on investment recommendations from these service providers without recognizing the potential conflict.
Service provider with affiliated brokerage arm	The service provider may advise plans to select investment funds that use the services of its affiliated brokerage arm, which results in greater revenue to the affiliate and, potentially, the service provider. Representatives from advisory firms we interviewed provided the following example:

Table 4. (Continued)

Source of potential conflict from affiliated businesses	Potential conflict of interest
	• A service provider with an affiliated brokerage arm only recommends investment funds that use the services of its brokerage arm; likewise, the investment fund provider uses a specific brokerage firm in order to win favorable recommendations from the brokerage firm's affiliated service provider. Such arrangements may not be disclosed to plan sponsors or participants. In a 2009 case, SEC found that a service provider with an affiliated brokerage arm advised its pension plan clients, including 401(k) plans, to direct their investment fund providers to execute trades through the affiliated brokerage arm.[b] Although this arrangement resulted in significantly higher revenue to both the service provider and the affiliate, the service provider did not disclose the conflict of interest as required.

Source: GAO analysis based on information from industry practitioners and an SEC enforcement case.

Note: A conflict of interest may or may not be a violation of ERISA or applicable securities laws, depending on the facts and circumstances.

[a] For more information on QDIAs, see a forthcoming GAO report.

[b] In the Matter of Merrill Lynch, Pierce, Fenner, and Smith, Inc., Investment Advisers Act Release No. 2834 (January 30, 2009). The firm agreed to settle charges with SEC and pay a civil money penalty of $1 million.

Many Service Providers Are Reported to Arrange Their Association with Plan Sponsors in a Manner That Avoids ERISA Fiduciary Responsibility

Although service providers that are subject to ERISA fiduciary standards are prohibited from benefiting from the investment of plan assets, many service providers that assist in selecting investment options are reported to structure their relationships with plans to avoid being subject to these standards. Under ERISA, a person who provides investment advice for direct or indirect compensation is a fiduciary; however, the EBSA regulations currently in effect establish a five-part test, each part of which must be met, to determine if a service provider is a fiduciary for purposes of providing investment advice.[39] Many industry experts we spoke with said that service providers often do not meet one or more parts of the test and thus avoid being subject to ERISA fiduciary standards. Consequently, these service providers may have a conflict of interest by increasing their compensation based on the funds selected by the plan without violating ERISA. Service providers may structure their association with a 401(k) plan to avoid meeting one or more parts of the current five-part test, as shown in figure 4. For example, an ERISA attorney said that although service providers give investment recommendations, they will include a provision in their contract that states that the investment recommendations provided are not intended to be the primary basis for decision making. A recent report by Labor's OIG found that some service providers included in their review and identified to have significant undisclosed conflicts of interest attempted to avoid meeting the criteria for ERISA fiduciary status under the current five-part test by simply stating in their investment adviser contract that they were not fiduciaries.[40] The 2010 report examined EBSA's handling of certain service providers, acting as pension consultants, that were determined by SEC in a 2005 staff report to have significant undisclosed conflicts of interest. According to the SEC report, many plan sponsors rely heavily on these pension consultants in making investment decisions. Other industry experts said that a service provider can avoid meeting the criteria of the five-part test if it offers investment recommendations as part of setting up the plan, rather than on a regular, recurring basis (see table 5). According to EBSA officials, it can easily be asserted by a service provider that advice given on a onetime basis does not meet the five-part test.[41]

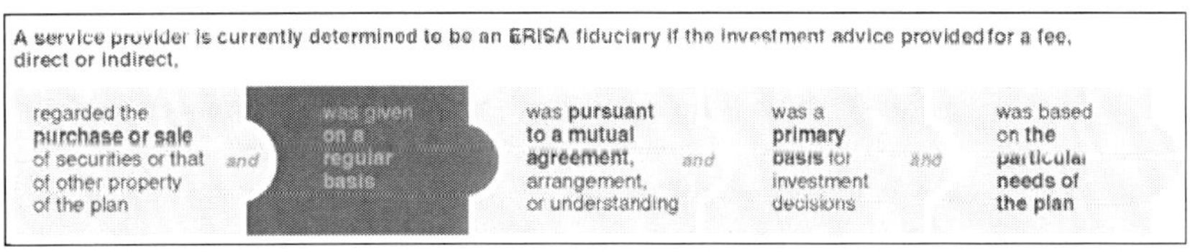

Source: GAO analysis of EBSA regulations.

Note: The current five-part test is reflected in EBSA's regulations. 29 C.F.R. § 2510.3-21(c).

Figure 4. 401(k) Service Provider May Fail to Be Deemed an ERISA Fiduciary for Purposes of Investment Advice by Not Meeting One Part of EBSA's Current Five-Part Test.

Table 5. Potential Conflict of Interest Scenario for Investment Assistance Provided to Plan Sponsors

The following example describes how a service provider may steer plan sponsors to select investment funds in which the service provider has a conflict of interest without giving formal investment advice subject to ERISA fiduciary standards: • A plan sponsor works with a service provider to establish a 401(k) plan. The service provider presents investment fund options to the plan sponsor for consideration, but does not formally recommend the selection of any particular investment fund. The plan sponsor will select 20 funds to offer in the 401(k) plan. • The service provider representative can receive compensation, such as through 12b-1 fees or a sales load, from these funds and selects those 20 funds that provide the highest payments for the plan's consideration. • The representative does not consider himself to be acting as an ERISA fiduciary because the plan sponsor makes the final decision about which investment options to include in the plan. Alternatively, the representative may provide a larger pool of funds (e.g., 50 funds) for the plan's consideration. Although the plan sponsor selects from a larger pool of funds, the service provider still has a conflict of interest because the representative chooses the 50 funds that provide the highest payments.

Source: GAO example based on information from industry practitioners.

When selecting investment options for the plan, plan sponsors can work with various types of service providers subject to different regulations, some of which may not be required to provide advice in the best interest of the plan or disclose conflicts of interest. Several industry experts we interviewed said that while some plan sponsors hire registered investment advisers (RIA) who are subject to SEC regulations and often acknowledge ERISA fiduciary responsibility, many other plan sponsors work with broker-dealer or insurance company representatives who are not subject to ERISA fiduciary responsibility and may also not be subject to SEC regulations. Under the Advisers Act, RIAs must seek to avoid conflicts of interest and, at a minimum, make full disclosure of material conflicts of interest.[42] However, other service providers, such as insurance company representatives, may not be subject to ERISA fiduciary duty or certain SEC regulations and thus may not be required to make recommendations in the best interest of their clients, or to disclose all conflicts of interest.[43] Furthermore, plan sponsors may contract directly with a bundled service provider that offers its own investment funds and does not provide formal investment advice subject to ERISA or SEC regulations.

No comprehensive data are available to determine how many service providers are ERISA fiduciaries for purposes of providing investment advice. Although plan sponsors are required to provide certain information about the plan and service providers in annual filings to EBSA, this information does not include which service providers are acting as ERISA fiduciaries. As we previously reported, ERISA requires that at least one fiduciary be named in the plan documents provided to participants, although others may be identified voluntarily.[44] Consequently, determinations as to ERISA fiduciary status of service providers may not be made unless an investigation by EBSA is initiated or a lawsuit is filed claiming that the plan has been harmed. Misunderstanding can also occur because many large providers offer a range of services that a sponsor can choose from, including some that involve fiduciary duties and others that may not.[45]

Despite reports indicating that many service providers are not acting as ERISA fiduciaries in providing investment assistance, industry experts and EBSA field investigators told us that plan sponsors are often not aware when a service provider is not an ERISA fiduciary and often assume the advice they receive from them is subject to these standards.[46] Consequently, plan sponsors may not be aware that service providers can have a financial incentive to recommend certain funds that would be prohibited if they were ERISA fiduciaries. As we previously reported, plan sponsors may also assume they have delegated all of their fiduciary duties to an outside professional hired to run the plan, even though the sponsor always retains some fiduciary obligation.[47] Several industry experts we spoke with, including EBSA field investigators, indicated that there is a considerable amount of confusion among plan sponsors about whether or not they are receiving investment advice subject to ERISA fiduciary standards. For example, unless disclosed on the schedule A of the annual form 5500, they noted that, in their opinion, plan sponsors are generally not aware, when dealing with service providers who are broker-dealers or insurance company representatives, that the providers are not giving formal investment advice subject to ERISA fiduciary standards and thus may be earning sales-based compensation on fund sales. Contributing to the confusion, broker-dealers or insurance company representatives can refer to themselves as advisers even though they are not providing advice as ERISA fiduciaries and are receiving sales-based compensation.[48] A service provider representative said that, from the plan sponsor's perspective, investment assistance provided by a nonfiduciary service provider that may have conflicts of interest often looks very similar to investment advice provided by an independent service provider with no ties to investment funds.

Smaller plans may be more exposed to conflicts of interest on the part of service providers because they are less likely than larger plans to receive investment assistance from a service provider that is acting as a fiduciary.

Several industry experts we spoke with said that larger plans are much more likely to employ RIAs who are subject to fiduciary standards under the Advisers Act in providing investment advice. Larger plans may also have sufficient resources and in-house expertise to make investment decisions without assistance. Smaller plans, on the other hand, often lack the resources to perform these tasks in-house or to hire an independent adviser who will act as an ERISA fiduciary. Smaller plans also often receive investment assistance from insurance brokers or broker-dealers, who are not acting as ERISA fiduciaries and also may not be subject to fiduciary standards under the Advisers Act, which requires the adviser to act solely in the best interests of the client.[49]

Conflicts of Interest in the Selection of Investment Options May Cause Problems for Plan Sponsors and Reduce Participants' Savings for Retirement

The potential conflicts of interest described by industry experts we interviewed could cause problems for plan sponsors if appropriate action is not taken. Under ERISA, plan sponsors are obligated to take steps to identify and address service providers' potential conflicts of interest and ensure that the plan is run in the best interest of participants.[50] For example, an advisory opinion issued by EBSA describes conditions under which revenue-sharing payments received by a fiduciary are permissible under ERISA. Specifically, the advisory opinion states that, in order for a fiduciary to avoid a prohibited transaction, revenue-sharing payments should be fully disclosed to the plan and used either to offset fees the plan is obligated to pay, on a dollar-for-dollar basis, or else be rebated to the plan.[51] In addition, EBSA and SEC developed a list of questions to assist plan sponsors with identifying and assessing service providers' potential conflicts of interest that is available on SEC's Web site.[52] The questions include inquiries about a service provider's compensation, affiliations, or other business relationships with money managers, and ERISA fiduciary status. Representatives of service providers and ERISA attorneys we spoke with also described steps plan sponsors could take to address service providers' potential conflicts of interest. For example, plan sponsors could

- examine a service provider's direct and indirect compensation,
- ensure that the investment options offered are diversified and not entirely composed of the service provider's proprietary funds,

- negotiate for institutional fund share classes which do not have revenue-sharing payments so that fees are paid through direct charges to the plan,[53] or
- specify in their contract that the service provider will not receive any compensation other than what is allowed for in the contract.

Although plan sponsors may take steps to address potential conflicts of interest, several industry experts we spoke with said that the complexity of service providers' business arrangements and insufficient disclosures pose challenges to plan sponsors who want to obtain information regarding potential conflicts. Some of these conflicts might rise to the level of a prohibited transaction, such as self-dealing. Even though revenue sharing is reported to be a widespread practice among 401(k) service providers, several industry experts we spoke with said that plan sponsors, especially of smaller plans, may not fully understand or even be aware of these payments. Further, some industry experts said that even if disclosures are provided, they are very complicated and difficult to understand.

If not addressed, conflicts of interest could lead to 401(k) plans offering investment funds with higher fees or mediocre performance, which can substantially reduce the amount of savings available for retirement. A service provider with a conflict of interest may steer plan sponsors toward investment funds that increase the service provider's compensation even if other funds with better performance are available at equal or lower cost. Several industry experts we interviewed said that the financial impact of conflicts of interest can be considerable. For example, representatives from one service provider we interviewed said fees for plans that have been managed by service providers with conflicts of interest can be reduced by 30 percent or more. Similarly, a representative from an advisory firm that does not accept payments from investment funds said that, in some cases, fees for the firm's 401(k) plan clients are reduced by 180 bps or more. As we previously reported, however, a detailed financial audit would be necessary to precisely estimate the financial impact of a conflict of interest in a specific situation.[54] While the financial harm from conflicted investment advice is difficult to estimate, several studies provide a general sense of the magnitude of the effect of an increase in fees for retirement savings over a worker's career. Based on a 1 percentage point increase in fees, projections from EBSA, a prior GAO report, and an industry study range from a 17 to 28 percent decline in final account balances.[55] The size of the impact varies based on the time horizon, the projected rate of return, and other assumptions made in the projection.

PARTICIPANTS MAY RECEIVE CONFLICTED INVESTMENT EDUCATION AND ADVICE FROM SERVICE PROVIDERS IN CERTAIN CIRCUMSTANCES, BUT ENHANCED DISCLOSURE COULD HELP MITIGATE SUCH CONFLICTS

Participants May Perceive Investment Education as Advice and May be Unaware of Situations When Service Providers Have Conflicts of Interest

Participants may be unaware that service providers, when furnishing education, may have financial interests in the investment options available to participants. For example, investment education, which may be provided to participants in brochures, other written materials, and computer models, can include asset allocation models that highlight specific investment options as examples of investments available under an asset class.[56] In particular, funds in which the service provider has a financial interest can be highlighted and participants may perceive this information as investment advice. In one case, representatives from a service provider for many large 401(k) plans told us that because the company can highlight its own funds as examples of investment options under each asset class through investor education, it has no plans to offer investment advice. While investment advice is subject to ERISA fiduciary standards, which require that the advice must be in the participant's best interest and prohibit the adviser from having a financial interest in the investment options recommended, investment education is not subject to these standards.[57] Thus, a provider furnishing education may do so despite a conflict of interest, such as a financial stake in the outcome of participants' investment decisions. EBSA requires providers who highlight proprietary funds as part of an asset allocation model to provide a statement that other investment options may be available under a plan; however, this statement may not sufficiently prevent participants from construing information on investment alternatives as advice.[58] For example, the statement is not required to explain that the service provider is not providing advice as an ERISA fiduciary who is required to act in the participants' best interests, and the provider may stand to profit from participants' investment decisions. Consequently, without the benefit of an enhanced disclaimer that explicitly states that the highlighted funds are not advice and that the service provider may have a financial interest in the funds, participants may believe that providers are giving investment advice that is in participants' best interests, even in situations where this may not be the case.

In addition to furnishing asset allocation models, some service providers may highlight specific investment funds in communications with participants, as part of providing investment education, by using language such as "you may wish to consider [this investment fund]" instead of "I recommend," which makes a subtle differentiation between investment education and advice that most participants will not understand. Moreover, agency field investigators said that service providers who avoid rendering formal investment advice subject to ERISA fiduciary standards may, nonetheless, refer to themselves as investment advisers to participants. Participants who confuse investment education for impartial advice may choose investments that do not meet their needs, pay higher fees than with other investment options, and have lower savings available for retirement.

Although several industry professionals said that providing investment advice to participants through computer models, subject to ERISA standards, has advantages in addressing potential conflicts of interest, others said that these models could have biases that are difficult to detect. While investment advice—through a direct service arrangement—can be provided to participants through a computer model from a service provider that does not have any affiliations with the investment options offered, two other computer model arrangements are permitted, the SunAmerica and the Pension Protection Act (PPA) eligible investment advice arrangements, in cases where the service provider may have a conflict of interest (see table 6). See appendix II for more information regarding the common formats providers use to deliver investment education and advice.[59]

Table 6. Types of Investment Advice Arrangements and Computer Models

Advisory opinions, guidance by EBSA, and the Pension Protection Act of 2006 set forth additional arrangements for investment advice that may be provided—by service providers if they meet applicable requirements—to plan participants in specified circumstances:

- **SunAmerica advice arrangement**—in December 2001, EBSA issued an advisory opinion (2001-09A), in response to a request by SunAmerica Retirement Markets Inc., asking if a retirement plan provider could hire an independent third party to provide participants in a 401(k) plan with investment advice using asset allocation models. EBSA, in the advisory opinion, specified that such advice arrangements were allowed as long as certain requirements were met. For example,[a]
  - The asset allocation model must be developed and maintained by an independent financial expert.
  - The advice arrangement must preserve the financial expert's ability to develop the model portfolios solely in the interest of the plan participants and beneficiaries.
  - Participants have the option to implement or disregard the investment advice generated by the model.

Table 6. (Continued)

• **Pension Protection Act's eligible investment advice arrangements**—Section 601 of the PPA provided two eligible investment advice arrangements (EIAA)—in the form of statutory exemptions from ERISA's prohibited transaction rules—for fiduciaries who might otherwise have conflicts of interest when rendering investment advice: (1) computer model-based advice arrangements and (2) level fee-based advice arrangements. For both types of arrangements, PPA provisions set forth compliance requirements. In addition, EBSA has proposed regulations pursuant to the PPA to outline additional technical requirements for PPA EIAAs. 75 Fed. Reg. 9,360. • PPA computer model arrangement—advice may be provided to participants or beneficiaries using a computer model that, among other things, is certified by an eligible investment expert and audited annually by an independent auditor.[b] PPA fee-leveling arrangement—advice may be provided to participants or beneficiaries by an adviser whose compensation does not vary depending on the basis of any investment option selected by plan participants or beneficiaries. This advice arrangement must be audited annually by an independent auditor. Labor has stated (see Field Assistance Bulletin No. 2007-01) that such requirements do not extend to fiduciaries' affiliates.

Source: GAO review of the PPA and EBSA regulations and materials.

[a] The requirements listed above are just a few examples of the requirements detailed in EBSA's Advisory Opinion. See advisory opinion 2001-09A for a complete list of requirements.

[b] According to the proposed regulations, the computer model must also (1) apply generally accepted investment theories that take into account the historic returns of different asset classes over defined periods of time; (2) utilize relevant information about the participant, which may include age, life expectancy, retirement age, and risk tolerance; (3) utilize prescribed objective criteria to provide asset allocation portfolios composed of investment options available under the plan; (4) operate in a manner that is not biased in favor of investments offered by the fiduciary adviser or a person with material affiliation or contractual relationship with the fiduciary adviser; and (5) take into account all investment options under the plan in specifying how a participant's account balance should be invested and is not inappropriately weighted with respect to any investment option.

Several industry professionals we interviewed said these models ensure consistency in the content of the advice rendered to multiple participants. In addition, unlike a one-on-one consultation or group presentation, a computer model may be audited to determine whether it is generating impartial information.[60] Despite these advantages of computer model-based advice, other industry professionals said that it is possible to build biases into these models that may be difficult to detect. For example, a computer model may be designed to exclude certain types of investment options, which results in situations in which participants are receiving advice that does not include all investment options available to participants. In particular, representatives from one service provider told us that a computer model's exclusion of target date

BIN TRAVERLER FORM

Cut By: Hilda Qty 23 Date 10/19/26

Scanned By:__________ Qty_____ Date_______

Scanned Batch ID's

Notes / Exceptions

funds could allow a provider to steer participants toward investment options that charge higher fees, such as managed accounts.

Although a number of studies have been conducted about the availability of investment assistance for participants, these studies do not always discern whether participants are provided investment education or advice.[61] According to a poll of 401(k) plan sponsors and service providers that we conducted in coordination with the Society of Human Resource Management and the Society of Professional Asset-Managers and Record Keepers, investment education is more commonly offered to participants than investment advice, although many respondents offered both.[62] Among respondents, brochures or other written materials were one of the most commonly used formats for delivering education and advice. Computer modeling, including Web-based tools, was also one of the most common methods of delivery reported.

Conflicts of Interest May Arise from Compensation to Service Providers for Cross-Selling Financial Products outside of Retirement Plans to Participants

Several industry experts we spoke with said that conflicts of interest also arise for 401(k) service providers who sell nonplan products and services, such as IRA rollovers, to participants outside their 401(k) plan, a practice known as cross-selling, which can considerably increase the service provider's compensation. While IRAs may serve participants' retirement needs by assisting them in saving for retirement, industry professionals we spoke to had concerns about the manner in which providers cross-sell IRA rollovers and other products to participants. Cross-selling products outside of a plan to participants can substantially increase a service provider's compensation, which creates an incentive for the service provider to steer participants toward the purchase of these products even though such purchases may not serve the participants' best interests. For example, products offered outside a plan may not be well suited to participants' needs or participants may be able to secure lower fees by choosing investment funds within their plans comparable with products offered outside their plans.[63] Industry professionals we spoke with said that cross-selling IRA rollovers to participants, in particular, is an important source of income for service providers. For example, according to an industry professional, a service provider could earn $6,000 to $9,000 in fees from a participant's purchase of an IRA, compared with $50 to $100 in fees if the same participant were to invest in a fund within a plan.

Plan sponsors can take steps to preclude service providers from cross-selling nonplan products and services to plan participants. For example, some plan sponsors require their plans' service providers to sign nonsolicitation agreements that prevent the service providers from marketing nonplan products and services to participants, but such agreements may not be widely used among plan sponsors. In addition, some service providers do not directly cross-sell products and services outside of a 401(k) plan to participants unless the service providers obtain permission from plan sponsors to do so, or unless participants initiate the discussion with service providers and inquire about products and services that are outside of their plans' investment offerings. According to our poll of 401(k) plan sponsors and service providers, of the 475 SHRM respondents who sponsored a 401(k) plan, 30 respondents explicitly allowed providers to market, or cross-sell, nonplan products to participants. Among the 30 respondents who allowed providers to engage in cross-selling, IRA rollovers were the most common product marketed to participants. However, the extent of cross-selling may be greater than reflected by the poll responses because service providers may do so without explicit permission. An industry professional told us that many sponsors of small and midsized plans may not be aware that their providers are cross-selling nonplan products and services to plan participants; hence, sponsors would not know to ask their providers to stop cross-selling nonplan products to participants.

Available data on IRA rollovers indicate that many participants choose to roll their assets into an IRA rather than keep their assets in an existing plan or roll them into a new employer's plan. As shown in figure 5, from 1998 to 2007, more than 80 percent of funds flowing into IRAs came from rollovers of lump-sum payments or account balances from defined benefit and defined contribution plans.[64]

According to data collected in 2006 from the Survey of Income and Program Participation, a survey relating to income and related information conducted by the U.S. Census Bureau, approximately 69 percent—or approximately 4.87 million—survey respondents who received a lump-sum distribution from their retirement plans rolled their distributed funds into IRAs.[65] Additionally, as shown in table 7, data from three large service providers indicate that, among participants who terminated their DC plan, between 42 and 48 percent of participants' plan assets were rolled into IRAs in the observed time periods.

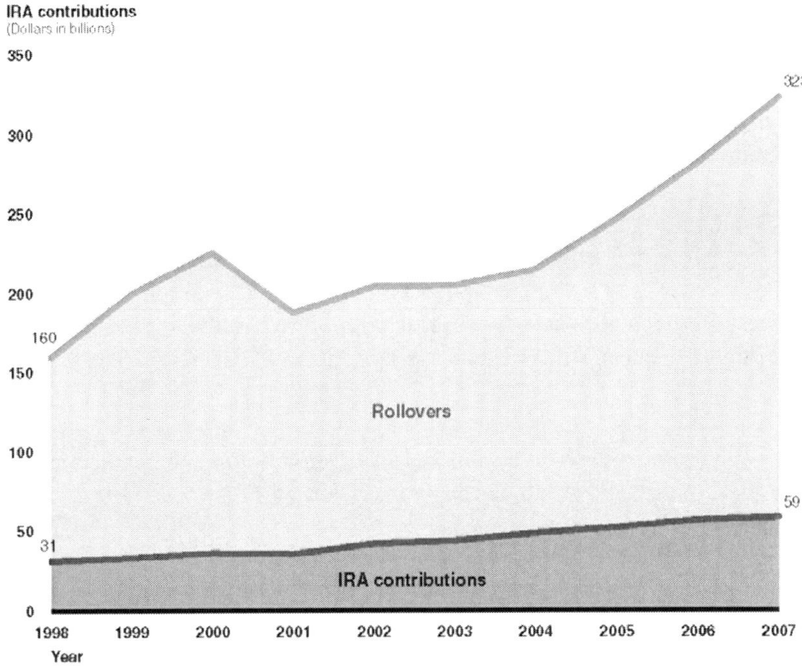

Source: Investment Company Institute.

Figure 5. IRA Assets from Contributions and Rollovers, 1998 to 2007.

An advisory opinion issued by EBSA states that ERISA fiduciary standards do not apply to a service provider cross-selling an IRA rollover to a participant unless the service provider is already servicing the plan as an ERISA fiduciary.[66] Consequently, unless the service provider is already an ERISA fiduciary, the service provider may advise a participant to roll his or her account funds into an IRA, even if such a transaction may not be in a participant's best interest. Without disclosures that indicate whether the service provider's assistance is subject to ERISA fiduciary standards and whether the service provider has a financial interest in the investment products, participants may mistakenly assume that service providers are required to act in the participant's best interest.[67] Furthermore, while final regulations may require a service provider to furnish IRA fee disclosures—such as a disclosure statement or a fee schedule—to participants, ERISA does not impose similar disclosure requirements for IRAs. In particular, service providers are not required to provide fee disclosures that specifically alert participants to the difference in fees between comparable funds available in their plan and funds offered by the plan's service provider. As we reported in 2009, owners of IRAs generally pay higher fees than participants in 401(k) plans because an individual IRA's account balance is usually not big enough to purchase an amount of investments large enough to qualify for volume discounts on fees.[68] Representatives from a 401(k) record-keeping firm said that, typically, IRA owners pay higher fees in the range of 25 to 30 bps and, in some cases, as high as 65 bps, which can be two to three times higher than fees paid by plan participants for in-plan investments. As a result of the lack of disclosure requirements on fees associated with IRAs, participants may be unaware of the higher fees associated with IRAs' rollovers and may not understand that paying these higher fees can reduce their retirement savings over time.

Table 7. Trends in Distribution of Defined Contribution Plan Assets when Participants Terminate Their Plans

(percent)			
	Service provider 1[a] 03/2005 to 05/2010	**Service provider 2[b] 01/2008 to 03/2009**	**Service provider 3[c] calendar year 2008**
Rolled funds into IRAs	48	43	42
Took cash or other distributions	11	8	6
Took other forms of distributions	0	2	2
Moved funds into new employers' plans	3	4	0
Remained in former employers' plans	38	43	50

Source: GAO review of proprietary data from three plan service providers.

[a] Data based on 976,600 terminated participants in service provider 1's retirement plan services from 03/01/2005 to 05/31/2010.

[b] Data based on 9,790 terminated participants in service provider 2's retirement plan services 401(k) plans from 01/01/2008 to 03/31/2009.

[c] Reported data among participants with termination dates in service provider 3's retirement plan services in 2008. The universe consists of more than 2,200 qualified plans and more than 3 million participants.

In March 2010, EBSA proposed a regulation that may improve fee disclosure to participants by requiring ERISA fiduciary advisers to disclose all fees or other compensation that they or their affiliates might receive in connection with an IRA rollover before providing investment advice on investment options for rollovers.[69] However, the requirements would not apply to nonfiduciaries that are providing advice to participants about IRA rollovers or inform participants that fees for IRAs may actually be higher than fees for investments in a plan. The U.S. Department of the Treasury (Treasury) has proposed a separate regulation to require advisers to provide notice to plan participants about the consequences of taking money out of a retirement plan.[70] Specifically, the disclosure would state that, among other things, investment options available in a plan may not be available for the same costs outside of a plan. However, without more explicit disclosure that IRAs typically have higher fees than investments in a plan, participants may not understand the difference in fees between IRAs and investments in a plan or the implication of higher fees on retirement savings over time.

EBSA's Enforcement Program and Recent Regulatory Actions Take Steps to Address the Potential for Conflicted Investment Advice, but Further Changes Could Better Address Conflicts of Interest

EBSA's Enforcement Efforts Do Not Address Potential Conflicts of Interest of Nonfiduciary Service Providers Involving the Selection of Investment Options

EBSA's enforcement efforts regarding potential conflicts of interest related to investment advice have not addressed potential violations by non-ERISA fiduciary service providers.[71] As we have previously reported, EBSA's ability to recover losses related to conflicts of interest by a service provider through its enforcement program is largely limited by the extent to which the service provider functions as a fiduciary under ERISA. For EBSA to take action against an individual or entity, there generally must be a breach of that fiduciary duty.[72] This can be an obstacle for EBSA given that many service providers structure their contracts with plans to attempt to avoid meeting one or more of the five parts of the current ERISA fiduciary definition reflected in EBSA regulations.[73] EBSA officials noted that it was rare to find a pension consultant to an employee benefit plan who acknowledged ERISA fiduciary status. Moreover, EBSA officials told us that proving ERISA fiduciary status under the five-part test tends to be a difficult and complex task because it depends on the facts an circumstances of each case. These cases are usually very resource-intensive and involve interviewing plan sponsors and service providers and reviewing a significant amount of documentation, which may need to be subpoenaed.[74] If EBSA is unable to determine that the service provider was an ERISA fiduciary pursuant to the five-part test currently in effect, or was otherwise an ERISA fiduciary, EBSA officials told us that they have the authority to cite plan sponsors or other plan fiduciaries to take corrective action for not prudently selecting and monitoring their service providers. However, according to Labor's OIG officials, EBSA does not focus its enforcement activities on plan sponsors or other plan fiduciaries that fail to detect conflicts of interest on the part of nonfiduciaries.[75]

Indeed, although EBSA has taken steps to address conflicted investment advice provided to plan sponsors or other plan fiduciaries by establishing the Consultant/Adviser Project (CAP), this effort is constrained by the current definition of an ERISA fiduciary investment adviser in its regulations. EBSA launched CAP, a national enforcement effort, at the beginning of fiscal year 2007 to investigate situations where ERISA fiduciary pension consultants or advisers may have used positions of trust with pension plans to generate improper, undisclosed fees for themselves or their affiliates. Since its launch, EBSA has designated 40 CAP cases and, as of August 2010, closed 16.[76] Of these 16 cases, only 5 yielded results, including restoration of plan assets and actions taken by ERISA fiduciaries to ensure that the conflicts of interest did not occur again. However, EBSA was unable to take action in other closed cases because it was unable to prove that service providers were ERISA fiduciaries under the five-part test or acted otherwise as fiduciaries. For example, EBSA investigated 12 of the 13 pension consultants identified in a 2005 SEC staff report for failing to disclose significant ongoing conflicts of interest to their pension fund clients[77]—all 13 of which were considered fiduciaries under the Advisers Act, which was used as a criterion in the SEC review—but EBSA told us that many of the 13 pension consultants were adept at avoiding fiduciary status under EBSA's five-part test. As a result, Labor's OIG recently reported that EBSA was only able to take action on 2 of these 13 consultants because only those 2 consultants were determined to be ERISA fiduciaries and were engaged in prohibited transactions.[78] The OIG report noted that without establishing ERISA fiduciary status, EBSA was unable to enforce conflict of interest issues and did not take any further action on these cases.

EBSA's Approach for Initiating Enforcement Cases May Also Fail to Detect Some Conflict of Interest Violations by ERISA Fiduciaries

EBSA's enforcement efforts through CAP may also miss violations by some ERISA fiduciaries because EBSA's approach for detecting violations does not currently include routine compliance examinations, which could help identify these violations. We reported in 2007 that EBSA does not conduct routine compliance examinations to focus its enforcement efforts the way other agencies do, and as a result, EBSA is not positioned to focus its resources on key areas of noncompliance or have adequate measurable performance goals to evaluate its impact on improving industry compliance.[79] For example, EBSA officials told us that they do not assess overall service provider compliance with the SunAmerica advisory opinion, which describes an appropriate method for providing one form of advice to participants,[80] and that they do not plan to assess compliance with the Pension Protection Act's eligible investment advice arrangement provisions after they are finalized.[81] Instead of routine compliance examinations, CAP cases have been initiated based on a variety of sources, including referrals from other agencies, spin-offs from regular enforcement cases, tips, and media reports. According to EBSA, 18 of the 40 initiated CAP cases were based on referrals from external sources, including the SEC staff report. While these leads may be specific and detailed, EBSA may not be able to rely on consistent referrals from these external sources because they may not always review the same topics. For example, many of SEC's referrals to EBSA, which resulted in CAP cases, stemmed from a onetime review by SEC of pension consultants in 2005.[82] In addition, 9 CAP cases were initiated by EBSA investigators based on leads from the media and participant complaints. While these sources are important, such methods may not reveal violations that are more complex or hidden. For example, it may be difficult for participants to detect conflict of interest violations and submit complaints to EBSA, since service providers' business arrangements may be complicated and their disclosures may be insufficient or difficult to understand.[83] Finally, Labor's OIG told us that EBSA does not have a formal process for looking at conflicts of interest regarding nonfiduciary service providers during EBSA's regular enforcement investigations—neither at the front end, when a plan hires a service provider, nor later on during transactions of plan assets. If EBSA's investigators come across a potential conflict of interest violation during their regular enforcement efforts, EBSA officials told us that the investigators refer the conflict of interest portion of the investigation to the CAP program. However, officials from Labor's OIG told us that, even though there have been numerous cases referred to the CAP program in this manner, as of July 2010, none had progressed to a CAP case in which EBSA took action against a service provider.[84]

To address such limitations, we previously recommended EBSA consider conducting routine compliance examinations.[85] Specifically, we recommended that EBSA evaluate the extent to which it could supplement its current enforcement practices with strategies used by similar agencies, such as routine compliance examinations and dedicating staff for risk management. EBSA officials told us that, starting in fiscal year 2011, they will implement routine compliance examinations.

Labor's Recent and Proposed Regulations Address Some of the Potential for Conflicts of Interest in Investment Advice and Lack of Disclosure

In addition to its enforcement efforts, EBSA has recently announced several regulatory initiatives that would address some potential conflicts of interest on the part of service providers. These efforts include (1) revising the definition of an ERISA fiduciary, (2) requiring enhanced disclosure of providers' direct or indirect compensation and fiduciary status, and (3) establishing safeguards for PPA investment advice arrangements. If the requirements specified in these regulations are implemented as they are currently written, they may help EBSA and plan sponsors detect and deter conflicted investment advice, but plan sponsors and participants still would not have sufficient and comparable information to identify potential conflicts of interest because disclosures are not required to be provided in a consistent and summary format.

Fiduciary Definition Regulations

Proposed regulations by EBSA to amend the definition of an ERISA fiduciary for purposes of investment advice, if implemented, would help address potential conflicts of interest on the part of service providers by encompassing a greater number of advisory relationships in which the plan sponsor relies on the service provider when making investment decisions.[86] Existing regulations have been in effect for 35 years, and EBSA officials told us they need to be revised based on knowledge and experience EBSA has gained through its enforcement efforts, as well as the evolution of the 401(k) industry.[87] In addition, a 2010 report by Labor's OIG noted that the five-part test is narrow and hampers EBSA's enforcement efforts. In place of the five-part test, the proposed regulation would establish ERISA fiduciary status based on a broader standard. In particular, the proposed regulation makes the following key changes, among others:

- Acknowledgment or representation as an ERISA fiduciary is sufficient to result in ERISA fiduciary status.
- Advice does not need to be provided on a regular basis to be considered a fiduciary act.
- The parties do not need to have a mutual understanding that the advice will serve as a primary basis for plan investment decisions.

Fulfilling any of the independent and alternative conditions specified in the proposal would be sufficient to result in ERISA fiduciary status for purposes of investment advice.[88] By reducing the number of conditions that need to be met to be deemed an ERISA fiduciary, the proposed regulation would encompass a greater number of service providers assisting plan sponsors with selecting investment options. In addition, the revised standards more closely align with advisory relationships that industry experts and service providers told us plan sponsors rely on to make investment decisions. As a result, the proposed regulations should help reduce confusion on the part of plan sponsors, many of whom are reported to currently believe they are receiving impartial advice subject to ERISA fiduciary standards when this is not the case. Moreover, the regulation may aid EBSA's enforcement efforts regarding conflicted investment advice by simplifying the method EBSA uses to determine who is an ERISA fiduciary. In addition to amending the five part test, the proposed regulations also state that selling or marketing investment options to a plan sponsor does not constitute investment advice if it is disclosed in writing that the person is not undertaking to provide impartial investment advice.[89] However, the proposed regulation does not specify the format for this disclosure. Given that industry experts told us there is a considerable amount of confusion among plan sponsors about whether or not they are receiving investment advice subject to ERISA fiduciary standards, some plan sponsors may continue to be unaware of the distinction between ERISA fiduciary advice and sales or marketing activities without a requirement that this disclosure be made in a consistent and prominent manner. While the proposed regulations should result in a greater number of advisory relationships being subject to ERISA fiduciary standards, the regulation has yet to be finalized. If EBSA does not finalize this regulation and replace the five-part test, many service providers may continue to act outside of ERISA fiduciary standards and EBSA's enforcement efforts will remain limited.

Service Provider Disclosure Regulations

Interim final regulations released by EBSA in July 2010 require enhanced service provider disclosure of compensation and ERISA fiduciary status.[90] These regulations, effective on July 16, 2011, for both new and existing arrangements between service providers and ERISA plans, specify that a contract between a covered plan[91] and a covered service provider[92] is not reasonable unless certain disclosures are made to the responsible plan fiduciary.[93] Required disclosures include descriptions of the services to be provided to the plan and the compensation the provider expects to receive for those services. In addition, if service providers expect to provide ERISA fiduciary services to plans, they are required to make a statement to such effect.[94] Industry experts indicated that this regulation should help plan sponsors identify conflicts of interest and assess whether they are causing harm to participants' balances. In addition the new disclosure requirements will allow EBSA to exercise enforcement authority over service providers who refuse to disclose direct and indirect compensation.[95] As shown in table 8, disclosures required by this regulation would provide plan sponsors with valuable information and could enhance their ability to evaluate compensation arrangements and potential conflicts of interest.[96]

Table 8. Categories of Service Provider Disclosures Required under Interim Final EBSA Regulations Effective July 2011

Type of disclosure	Requirement[a]
Primary compensation disclosures	The service provider must describe all of the compensation it expects to receive.[b] For this purpose, the compensation will fall into one or more of the following four categories: • *Direct compensation*: a description of all direct compensation, either in the aggregate or by service, that the service provider reasonably expects to receive in connection with the covered plan. • *Indirect compensation*:[c] a description of all indirect compensation that the covered service provider reasonably expects to receive. The description must include identification of the services for which the indirect compensation will be received and identification of the payer of the indirect compensation.

Type of disclosure	Requirementa
	• *Compensation paid among related parties*: a description of any compensation that will be paid among the covered service provider, an affiliate, or a subcontractor if it is set on a transaction basis (e.g., commissions, soft dollars, finder's fees, or other similar incentive compensation based on business placed or retained) or charged directly against the covered plan's investments and reflected in the net value of the investments (e.g., 12b-1 fees). The description must include identification of the services for which the compensation will be paid and identification of the payers and recipients of the compensation (including the status of the payer or recipient as an affiliate or subcontractor). • *Compensation for termination of arrangement*: a description of any compensation that the service provider reasonably expects to receive in connection with termination of the contract or arrangement and how any prepaid amounts will be calculated and refunded upon such termination.
Additional disclosures for record-keeping services	In addition, if record-keeping services will be provided to the covered plan, a covered record-keeping service provider must give a description of all direct and indirect compensation that the covered service provider, affiliate, or subcontractor reasonably expects to receive in connection with the record-keeping services, and • if the covered service provider reasonably expects record-keeping services to be provided, in whole or in part, without explicit compensation for such record-keeping services, or • when compensation for record-keeping services is offset or rebated based on other compensation received. A reasonable and good faith estimate of the cost to the covered plan of such record-keeping services, including the following: • an explanation of the methodology and assumptions used to prepare the estimate, and • a detailed explanation of the record-keeping services that will be provided to the covered plan. Under this disclosure requirement, if a provider who is a record keeper receives other compensation (e.g., revenue such as subtransfer agency fees) and offsets it against its stated fee or gives credits against its record-
	keeping fees (e.g., for the use of mutual funds managed by affiliated managers), the record keeper must disclose to the responsible plan fiduciary the reasonable costs of the record-keeping services without the offsets or credits. Generally speaking, the reasonable cost is what the provider would charge for those services if there was no revenue sharing and if proprietary funds were not used.
Additional disclosures required for certain investments	*Fiduciary services*: In the case of a covered fiduciary service provider who manages a separate contract, product, or entity that holds plan assets, the provider must disclose the following information for each investment in which the plan has a direct equity interest, and for which fiduciary services will be provided:

Table 8. (Continued)

Type of disclosure	Requirement[a]
	• a description of any compensation that will be charged directly against the amount invested in connection with the acquisition, sale, or transfer of, or withdrawal from, the investment contract, product, or entity (e.g., sales loads, sales charges, deferred sales charges, redemption fees, surrender charges, exchange fees, account fees, and purchase fees); • a description of the annual operating expenses (e.g., expense ratio) —if the return on the investment is not fixed, and • a description of any ongoing expenses in addition to annual operating expenses (e.g., wrap fees, mortality and expense fees). *Record-keeping or brokerage services*: In the case of a covered service provider who provides record-keeping or brokerage services for a participant-directed plan with designated investment options, for each designated investment alternative for which record-keeping services or brokerage services will be provided, the same information must be provided as for fiduciaries (above).

Source: EBSA's Interim Final Regulations on Service Provider Disclosures: 75 Fed. Reg. 41,600.

[a] The disclosures must contain a description of the manner in which the compensation will be received, such as whether the plan will be billed or the compensation will be deducted directly from the covered plan's accounts or investments.

[b] Compensation is defined in the regulation as anything of monetary value, such as money, gifts, awards, and trips, but excluding nonmonetary items of $250 or less received during the term of the contract or arrangement.

[c] Indirect compensation is compensation that is received from any source other than the covered plan, the covered plan sponsor, the covered service provider, an affiliate of the service provider, or a subcontractor of the service provider.

While these disclosures may help plan sponsors and EBSA detect and deter conflicted investment advice, they may leave out important information that could help plan sponsors compare compensation arrangements and assess the potential for conflicts of interest. Specifically, the interim final regulations do not specify that these disclosures be made in any particular manner or format. As a result, the disclosures may be made through multiple documents, which could reduce their usefulness for plan sponsors and EBSA in detecting conflicts of interest given that, as industry experts told us, such disclosures can be very complicated and difficult to understand. As part of the comment process on these interim final regulations, EBSA solicited comments about the feasibility of requiring the disclosures to be reported in a consistent and summary format, such as taking the form of a summary document, limited to one or two pages, that would include key information intended to provide an overview for the responsible plan fiduciary of the information required to be disclosed.[97] The summary also would be required to include a road map for the plan fiduciary describing where to find the more detailed elements of the disclosures required by the regulation. EBSA plans to examine the comments received before it includes this kind of requirement in the final regulations. Without being presented in a consistent summary format, the disclosure regulations may not be as effective as intended.

Another limitation of these interim final regulations is that they do not require that service providers specifically disclose whether they have conflicts of interest. Since many conflicts result from the payment of money or other items of monetary value, EBSA and others have argued that the direct and indirect compensation disclosures required by this interim regulation will reveal some conflicts of interest. But, while these regulations may provide more compensation information to plan sponsors, Labor's OIG told us that the regulations do not necessarily ensure that plan sponsors understand how the compensation translates into business arrangements with potential conflicts of interest. In a recent report, Labor's OIG found that the disclosures required by EBSA's interim final regulation would not require that conflicts from two of the cases identified in the 2005 SEC study be disclosed. They pointed to these two cases as examples to show how conflicts of interest could go undetected under the interim final regulations. As a result, OIG recommended that EBSA require the disclosure of all conflicts of interest. In response, EBSA stated that it felt that the interim final regulation may already provide this requirement through the detailed disclosures of direct and indirect compensation and that it was in the process of providing clarifying interpretations. Given that plan sponsors must assess conflicts of interest when selecting service providers, it is important that such conflicts be clearly disclosed.

In addition, the interim final regulation requires service providers to disclose information to plan sponsors, but not participants.[98] While some of these disclosures may make it to participants through various communications by plan sponsors, complete information on service provider compensation is not readily available to participants. As an attempt to remedy this, EBSA also published final regulations on October 20, 2010, designed to improve participant-level fee disclosure by requiring that plan sponsors provide participants core information about investments available under the plan, including performance and fee information, in a chart or similar format designed to facilitate investment comparisons.[99]

PPA Eligible Investment Advice Arrangement Regulations

Many industry experts we interviewed said that investment advice arrangements permitted under the PPA should make investment advice more widely available to participants; however, some industry experts said the established safeguards may not sufficiently address potential conflicts of interests on the part of service providers. ERISA generally precludes service providers with conflicts of interest from furnishing investment advice. However, in an effort to expand the availability of investment advice to more participants, the PPA created two eligible investment advice arrangements that allow service providers who have a conflict of interest to furnish advice to plan participants. Specifically, under the PPA, an otherwise conflicted service provider may furnish investment advice using either a computer model arrangement or a level fee arrangement.

EBSA proposed regulations in March 2010 to administer these requirements of the PPA and received comments from industry professionals and other interested parties.[100] Several industry professionals and service providers submitted comments in support of EBSA's efforts to increase participants' access to unbiased investment advice and minimize the effects of service providers' potential conflicts of interests. However, some industry professionals we interviewed expressed concerns about whether the PPA advice arrangements sufficiently minimize the risks posed by service providers' conflicts of interest since it is possible to embed investment biases into computer models, which may be difficult to detect even when computer models are audited. For example, an industry representative said that adequate monitoring and auditing of computer models may be costly and that auditors may not be aware of the various ways in which computer models could be manipulated. In addition, computer models may be designed to exclude certain types of investment options, such as target date funds. If basic investment options offered in a plan are excluded from the computer model, the advice provided will be based on an incomplete analysis of investment options or holdings the participant may have in his or her 401(k) account. The exclusion of certain investment options from computer models may have the effect of steering participants toward options that may involve higher fees. Furthermore, even in the situation where a service provider's profits do not vary depending on participants' investment decisions, the service provider may nonetheless exhibit a natural bias toward its proprietary funds when furnishing fund recommendations to participants.

CONCLUSION

While there are no comprehensive data on the prevalence or impact of service providers' conflicts of interest, available evidence suggests that there are a broad range of potential conflicts of interests that may harm participants and beneficiaries. Numerous industry experts we spoke with identified a wide variety of arrangements, often, but not always, complex, where conflicts of interest can occur to the possible detriment of plans and their participants. The arrangements are often designed in a way that makes it difficult for conscientious plan sponsors to detect them. Participants rely on the plan and its fiduciaries to review the investment options and services provided through the plan. Given the potential for financial harm to participants, it is important to ensure that plan sponsors, as fiduciaries, are aware of whether a conflict of interest exists and that the actions of service providers are appropriate. Conflicts of interest related to the plan's investment options can negatively affect 401(k) participants through higher fees and lower investment returns, which, ultimately, reduce their income in retirement. When service providers stand to gain from a plan sponsor or participant's selection of investment options, it is important to ensure that those providers do not have an undue influence over the plan sponsor or participant's selection process—or participants' balances could suffer. However, the complexity of business arrangements with service providers presents significant challenges for plan sponsors to fulfill their obligation to identify and mitigate potential conflicts of interest and ensure that the plan is operated in the best interest of participants. This may be particularly problematic for smaller plans, which do not have the resources to hire an independent adviser to review their options. The presence of conflicts of interest and the potential for financial harm hinder participants' retirement security and call into question the integrity of the 401(k) system, and may undermine participants' trust and willingness to save for retirement.

EBSA has a pivotal role in helping plan sponsors ensure that plans are operated in participants' best interests. In order to make prudent investment decisions, plan sponsors and participants need to understand when a service provider is acting in the role of a salesperson rather than a fiduciary adviser, required by law to act in the best interests of the plan and its participants. It is especially important for plan sponsors and participants to know if a service provider stands to gain from the selection of particular investment options. EBSA has recently taken several important steps to address the potential for conflicts of interest in investment advice. In particular, EBSA's interim final regulations, which require service providers to give enhanced disclosure of compensation arrangements, could help plan sponsors more clearly identify potential conflicts of interest and the fiduciary status of service providers. These regulations should help address the challenges faced by plan sponsors and participants. However, unless the disclosures are presented in a format that allows for a consistent comparison across investment options, it will inhibit the effectiveness of these regulations. If changes are not made to current disclosures, plan sponsors will not be able to make meaningful comparisons among different funds and providers. In addition, given that EBSA's enforcement efforts for conflicts of interest focus on service providers rather than plan sponsors, EBSA should finalize its proposed regulations to revise the current five-part test to better ensure that service providers that recommend investment options are subject to ERISA's fiduciary standard, and enhance disclosure to plan sponsors when investment assistance is not impartial. If the five-part test is not changed, service providers may still make investment recommendations to plan sponsors without being subject to ERISA fiduciary standards, and EBSA's ability to take enforcement actions will continue to be limited. Moreover, if disclosures to plan sponsors are not required to be made in a consistent and prominent manner, some plan sponsors may continue to be unaware of the distinction between ERISA fiduciary advice and sales or marketing activities.

Additional measures are also needed to better ensure that participants are protected from the potential consequences of conflicted investment advice. To better ensure that participants are not improperly swayed by educational communications, requirements for guidance to participants on the difference between education and advice may need to be evaluated. Without a change in current standards, participants may continue to perceive education as advice and make decisions on the basis of information communicated by service providers with a financial interest in the investment funds. Improved disclosures may also be needed to help participants understand whether their service provider is acting as a salesperson rather than a fiduciary adviser when providing assistance to participants in acquiring financial products outside of the plan, such as an IRA rollover. Otherwise, participants will continue to be unaware if their plan's service provider is not required to provide advice in the best interest of the participant and may be earning a commission from these product sales. Efforts for improved disclosure may be strengthened through coordination with the Department of the Treasury on proposed regulations designed to help participants understand the potential consequences of moving assets outside of their plan. If no action is taken and conflicts of interest persist, participants' confidence and willingness to save in the 401(k) system may be weakened and an untold number of 401(k) participants may pay unnecessarily high costs, through investment fees and IRA rollovers; accrue lower investment returns; and have correspondingly less savings available for retirement.

RECOMMENDATIONS FOR EXECUTIVE ACTION

To better ensure that plan sponsors and participants can rely on impartial information in making investment decisions, we recommend that the Secretary of Labor direct the Assistant Secretary for EBSA to take the following actions:

- Amend and finalize proposed regulations to change the definition of a fiduciary for purposes of investment advice. Specifically, the Secretary should amend the proposed regulations to require that service providers' written disclosures specifying that they are not undertaking to provide impartial investment advice be provided to the plan sponsor in a consistent and prominent manner.
- Amend and finalize interim final regulations regarding disclosure of service providers' direct and indirect compensation from plan investments and fiduciary status to require that the information be provided in a consistent and summary format.
- Evaluate and revise Labor's interpretive bulletin on investment education, which is important in helping participants and beneficiaries make investment decisions. Specifically, in light of current practices, the Secretary should revise current standards, which permit a service provider to highlight certain investment alternatives, such as proprietary funds, which may result in greater revenue to the service provider, in educational materials. Labor could consider a variety of steps to address this potential conflict of interest, such as requiring service providers to disclose that they may have a financial interest in the options highlighted or prohibiting them from using proprietary funds as examples.
- Require that service providers, when assisting participants with the purchase of investment products offered outside of their plan, disclose in a consistent and prominent manner, either before or at the point of sale, any financial interests they may have in the outcomes of such transactions and inform participants as to whether their assistance is subject to ERISA fiduciary standards.

In addition, to better ensure that plan participants have sufficient information when deciding whether to move plan funds into investment alternatives outside their plan, we recommend that the Secretary of the Treasury amend the applicable requirements of its proposed disclosure rule to specifically require that service providers, when recommending the purchase of investment products outside retirement plans, inform plan participants that fees applicable outside their plans may be higher than fees applicable within their plans.

AGENCY COMMENTS AND OUR EVALUATION

We provided a draft of this report to the Department of Labor, SEC, and Treasury for their review. Treasury generally agreed with our recommendation to amend its proposed disclosure rule to specify that fees applicable for investment products outside of plans may be higher than fees applicable within plans. Treasury and SEC also provided technical comments, which we have incorporated where appropriate.

Overall, Labor generally agreed with our findings and to consider our recommendations as it conducts a review of these issues and evaluates public comments received on pending regulations. Labor noted that the interim final regulation to require enhanced disclosure of service providers' compensation arrangements represents significant progress and disagreed with our conclusion that these disclosures will not be effective unless they are presented in a format that allows for a consistent comparison across investment options. We concur that the disclosures required by this regulation would provide plan sponsors with valuable information and could enhance their ability to evaluate potential conflicts of interest. However, industry experts we spoke with noted that such disclosures can be very complicated and difficult to understand. Furthermore, as Labor has previously pointed out in the interim final rule regarding fee disclosure (75 Fed. Reg. 41,600), in the absence of a summary format, a service provider can fulfill this requirement by providing different documents from separate sources. Providing disclosures in multiple formats in different documents will inhibit the effectiveness of this regulation, particularly for plans that do not have the requisite expertise or the resources to hire an independent adviser to review their options.

Additionally, Labor noted that GAO did not conduct a cost-benefit analysis of recommendations to address potential conflicts of interest. GAO conducts its work in response to congressional requests for information and employs a variety of qualitative and quantitative methodologies in carrying out our mission. We choose these methodologies based on a variety of factors and constraints, such as the scope of our research objectives, availability of reliable data, costs and time constraints, as well as other considerations. We acknowledge that there are a number of options Labor could consider for the format of a summary disclosure and we agree that this requirement should be implemented at minimal cost to service providers and sponsors. We support Labor's following the appropriate administrative procedures in conducting its regulatory reviews and initiatives, including conducting a cost-benefit analysis. In this context, we wish to reiterate our past concerns about the harm plan participants can experience from undisclosed conflicts of interest. For example, as we reported in 2007, our analysis of available data on pension consultants and DB plans revealed a statistical association between inadequate disclosure of conflicts of interest and lower investment returns for ongoing plans. We also note that disclosing potential conflicts of interest in a manner that is readily apparent could benefit EBSA's oversight and enforcement efforts. Further, if Labor found the cost to service providers in preparing a summary document to be significant, this would also point to the difficulty that plan sponsors would have in extracting this information from multiple documents to obtain consistent information to allow for comparisons across different investment options and providers.

Labor also noted, regarding our recommendation to revise the interpretive bulletin on investment education, that current standards take a number of steps to limit the potential for abuse and Labor would need to evaluate several factors in considering any changes. While we concur that the interpretive bulletin includes several requirements to address the potential for conflicts of interest, it does not specifically alert participants when the service provider has a financial interest in investment options highlighted as examples, nor does it state that these examples do not constitute investment advice. Without an explicit disclaimer to this effect, participants may believe that providers are giving investment advice that is in participants' best interests, even in situations where this may not be the case. We look forward to Labor's evaluation of this issue and options to address it.

Finally, Labor noted that it may not have the authority to act on our recommendation to require service providers to disclose financial interests they may have in the sale of financial products outside of the plan, such as IRA rollovers. In the recently proposed regulation to amend the definition of an ERISA fiduciary, Labor noted concerns that participants may not be adequately protected from advisers who provide distribution recommendations that subordinate participants' interests to the advisers' own interests and solicited comments on possible actions to take to address this issue. We look forward to Labor's evaluation of whether or not it has the authority to address conflicts of interest related to the sale of financial products outside of the plan. If Labor determines that it does not have the authority to act in this area, it may be appropriate for Congress to consider possible legislative remedies. In the absence of any action to address this issue, participants may continue to be unaware when their plan's service provider stands to gain from the sale of IRA rollovers and other financial products outside of the plan.

Labor also provided technical comments on the draft report, which we have incorporated where appropriate.

Sincerely yours

Charles A. Jeszeck, Director
Education, Workforce and Income Security Issues

APPENDIX I. SCOPE AND METHODOLOGY

To determine the circumstances where conflicted investment advice may be provided to plan sponsors, we analyzed available research and documentation, including a report from the Securities and Exchange Commission (SEC), industry white papers, and documentation from the Department of Labor (Labor) and SEC cases pertaining to service provider conflicts of interest. We also interviewed industry professionals; pension consulting firms and other service providers; officials from Labor, SEC, the Department of the Treasury, the Financial Industry Regulatory Authority, and the Securities Industry and Financial Markets Association; and other relevant organizations. To determine how the fiduciary duty of the Employee Retirement Income Security Act of 1974 (ERISA) applies to investment advice provided to plan sponsors and the scope of ERISA's prohibited transactions rule, we reviewed relevant laws, including ERISA securities laws, regulations, and Labor advisory opinions, and interviewed industry professionals. As part of our research, we reviewed available information, including a report from Labor's Office of Inspector General, and conducted interviews with industry professionals and Labor officials to determine the extent to which advisers to plan sponsors are considered ERISA fiduciaries.

To determine the circumstances where conflicted investment advice may be provided to plan participants, we reviewed available literature and interviewed industry professionals and plan service providers. Additionally, we reviewed relevant statutes, including ERISA and the Pension Protection Act of 2006 (PPA), as well as regulations promulgated by Labor to understand where applicable law draws the distinction between investment education and advice. To determine what is known about the extent to which plan participants have access to investment education and advice, and to identify the common formats for furnishing such information, we reviewed available data from industry studies and conducted a poll of plan sponsors and service providers, as described below:

- We reviewed data from the Profit Sharing/401(k) Council of America's (PSCA) 2008 survey of retirement plans (published in 2009, but reflecting 2008 plan experience). The results of PSCA's 2008 survey are based on the experiences of 908 plans—including 28 profit-sharing plans, 607 401(k) plans, and 273 combination profit-sharing/401(k) plans—with 7.4 million participants. The plans that participated in PSCA's survey range in size from 1 participant to 5,000-plus participants. PSCA is a nonprofit association of 1,200 companies that sponsor defined contribution plans for 5 million employees. PSCA represents the interests of its members and offers assistance with profit-sharing and 401(k) plan design, administration, investment, compliance, and communication.
- In addition to reviewing industry data to assess the availability of investment education and advice for plan participants, we created an online questionnaire in coordination with the Society of Human Resource Management (SHRM) and the Society of Professional Asset-Managers and Record Keepers (SPARK). In the questionnaire, we asked plan sponsors that are members of SHRM and service providers that are members of SPARK whether investment education and advice are provided to plan participants, the format for delivering such information, and whether investment products and services unrelated to plans are marketed to participants. We implemented the Web-based questionnaire with SPARK members using our Web application, while SHRM implemented the questionnaire with its members using SHRM's Web application. SHRM and SPARK officials solicited responses from their members by distributing, to

their members, our e-mail introducing the study, describing the question topics, and directing members to an Internet address for the questions. SHRM and SPARK officials also sent out periodic reminders about the questionnaire over several weeks between July 2010 and August 2010. SHRM distributed the introductory e-mail among 2,698 of its members, and SPARK distributed the e-mail among its board members, which included representatives from every SPARK member organization (over 250 companies). In total, 700 members—627 from SHRM and 73 from SPARK—responded to the questionnaire. The survey results are not representative of the general plan sponsor and service provider populations because our respondent population excludes plan sponsors that are not members of SHRM and service providers that are not members of SPARK. Because of the methodological limitations associated with deploying these questions, information obtained represents only the views of the respondents, not the overall population of 401(k) plan sponsors and service providers. In addition, we took steps in the development of the questions to minimize the variability of survey results. Prior to administering the questionnaire, the questions were reviewed by an independent survey expert in our methodology group and officials from SHRM and SPARK. We made changes to the content and format of the questionnaire based on reviewers' feedback.

- To analyze the incidence of IRA rollovers among plan participants, a circumstance in which conflicted investment assistance may be provided to plan participants, we collected and analyzed industry data from three sources to determine the frequency with which plan participants are rolling plan funds into IRAs:
    - The Survey of Income and Program Participation (SIPP), which is a survey conducted by the U.S. Census Bureau. The main objective of the SIPP is to provide accurate and comprehensive information about the income and program participation of individuals and households in the United States. The SIPP is conducted on a continuous series of national panels, with durations from 2 ½ to 4 years, with sample size ranging from approximately 14,000 to 36,700 interviewed households. The SIPP sample is a multistage-stratified sample of the U.S. civilian, noninstitutionalized population. We used data from the 2004 topical module 7 survey and extracted survey responses to

determine the percentage of survey respondents who took cash distributions from their retirement plans and rolled distributed funds into individual retirement accounts (IRA). In particular, we used variables EPREVLMP (for survey respondents who have ever received a lump-sum payment from a pension or retirement plan from a previous job, including any lump sums that may have been directly rolled over to another plan or to an IRA) and ELMPWHER, answer choice IRA (for survey respondents who rolled lump-sum payments into IRAs). The 2004 SIPP survey results are based on responses from people surveyed in different waves over a 2 ½-year period, with survey interviews lasting into 2006. Specifically, for wave 7, interviews were conducted from February 2006 to May 2006. Results are generalizable to the population at the time of survey.

- The Investment Company Institute (ICI) is the national association of U.S. investment companies, and it works to promote public understanding of mutual funds and other investment companies. ICI publishes statistics on the U.S. retirement market every quarter as an information resource for mutual fund companies, the media, policymakers, and researchers. ICI combines data from its own mutual fund survey database and from other trade associations with data from the U.S. Department of Labor, the Federal Reserve Board, and the Internal Revenue Service (IRS) to compile detailed IRA asset information, including the portions of funds flowing into IRAs from rollovers and contributions. Total IRA market assets are derived from tabulations of total IRA assets provided by the IRS Statistics of Income Division for tax years 1989, 1993, 1996-2002, and 2004; with preliminary data provided for 2006 and 2007. Tabulations are based on a sample of IRS returns. GAO did not conduct any direct analysis of ICI data.
- Three service providers that service defined contribution plans also compiled proprietary data on what happens to plan participants' defined contribution plan funds when participants terminated their retirement plans. Results from service provider 1 were based on 976,600 terminated participants in the provider's defined contribution retirement plan services from March 1, 2005, through May 31, 2010. Results from service provider 2 were

> based on 9,790 terminated participants in the provider's retirement plan services 401(k) plans from January 1, 2008, through March 31, 2009. Results from service provider 3 were based on participants with termination dates in 2008. The universe consisted of more than 3 million participants from more than 2,200 plans. In addition, the proprietary data from plan service providers are not generalizable to the universe of retirement plan participants. However, the results are consistent with and corroborate each other.

We assessed the reliability of the data we present and found the data to be sufficiently reliable as used in this report. To describe the steps that Labor has taken to address conflicts of interest, we reviewed documentation of Labor's enforcement activities related to conflicted investment advice practices. We also reviewed past GAO and Labor Inspector General reports and interviewed Labor officials to evaluate the adequacy of Labor's enforcement efforts to prevent conflicted investment advice. In addition, we reviewed documentation from Labor and industry participants related to three recent or soon-to-be-released Labor regulations: (1) a proposed rule amending the definition of ERISA fiduciary duty regarding investment advice (published in October 2010), which would amend the regulatory definition of the fiduciary duty for plan investment advisers to include pension consultants and other plan advisers who do not fall under the current regulatory definition; (2) an interim final rule regarding service provider disclosures of direct and indirect compensation to plan sponsors (issued in July 2010); and (3) PPA eligible investment advice arrangements (issued in March 2010), which fall under a statutory exemption to the ERISA prohibited transactions rule. Finally, we interviewed Labor officials to discuss the scope of each regulation and key features that may mitigate conflicts of interest. We conducted our review from January 2010 through January 2011 in accordance with generally accepted government auditing standards. Those standards require that we plan and perform the audit to obtain sufficient, appropriate evidence to provide a reasonable basis for our findings and conclusions based on our audit objectives. We believe that the evidence obtained provides a reasonable basis for our findings and conclusions based on our audit objectives.

APPENDIX II. COMMON FORMATS FOR DELIVERING INVESTMENT EDUCATION AND ADVICE

Investment education and advice may be provided to participants in different formats, most commonly through brochures or other written materials and computer modeling. Other formats for providing education or advice include one-on-one sessions with service providers and seminars and workshops.

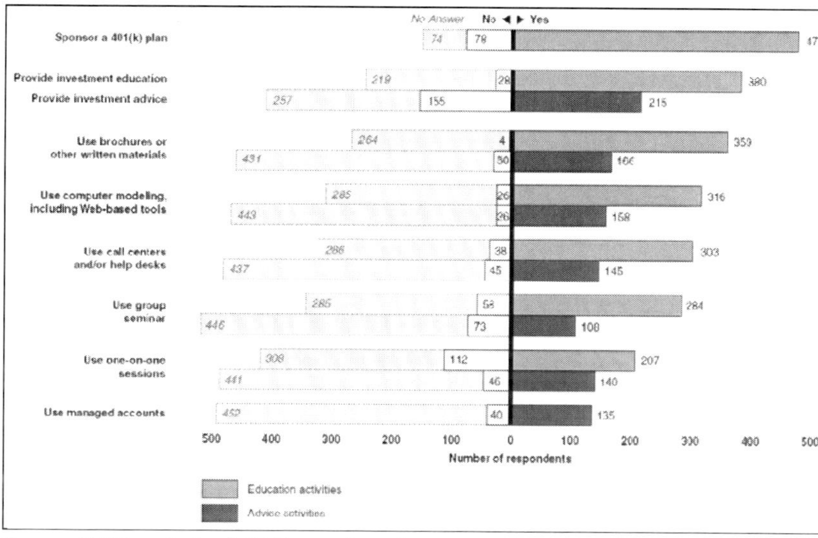

Source: GAO analysis of GAO questionnaire.

Figure 6. GAO Poll Results from SHRM Respondents.

A number of studies have been conducted about the availability of investment assistance for participants; however, these studies do not always discern whether participants are provided investment education or advice.[101] According to a poll of 401(k) plan sponsors and service providers that we conducted in coordination with SHRM and SPARK, investment education is more commonly offered than investment advice, although many respondents offered both.[102] As shown in figure 6, of the 475 SHRM respondents who sponsored a 401(k) plan, 380 provided investment education and 215 provided investment advice. Of these respondents, 202 provided both education and advice. Among respondents, brochures or other written materials were the most commonly used formats for delivering education and advice. Computer modeling, including Web-based tools, was the second most common method of delivery reported. Industry research by an organization of 401(k) and profit-sharing plans yielded similar results, with 51.8 percent of plans providing investment advice to plan participants and with 28.3 percent of participants using advice when it was offered.[103]

Among plans providing investment advice, the most common methods of delivery are one-on-one counseling sessions, Internet providers (including those with computer modeling programs), and telephone hotlines.[104] Industry survey results also indicate that smaller plans with fewer than 50 participants are more likely to use one-on-one counseling sessions, while larger plans of 5,000-plus participants tend to use Internet providers.[105]

APPENDIX III. TYPES OF COMPUTER MODEL ADVICE ARRANGEMENTS

Computer models can be used to render investment advice to participants in three different arrangements: (1) the direct service arrangement, (2) the SunAmerica arrangement, and (3) the PPA computer model arrangements. As shown in figure 7, the direct service arrangement is utilized when a plan sponsor contracts directly with an independent advisory firm, which develops a computer model that renders advice to plan participants. The independent advisory firm should not be affiliated with any investment fund or accept payments from funds that its model recommends as investment options. Accordingly, the firm should operate without a vested interest in its recommendations and not incur any conflicts of interest.

For advice arrangements where providers offer their own investment funds and thus have a conflict of interest, Labor has set forth specific requirements under which these providers may offer investment advice. As shown in figure 8, the SunAmerica arrangement allows the service provider to contract with an independent advisory firm to develop and administer a computer model to provide investment advice. Because the primary service provider may have a conflict of interest for certain investment options offered to participants, Labor requires that, among other things, the independent financial expert—who is not the primary service provider—develop and maintain the computer model that renders advice to participants solely in the interest of plan participants.

As shown in figure 9, the PPA computer model arrangement, on the other hand, allows the service provider to develop the computer model in-house, subject to certain requirements the PPA has established to address the service provider's conflict of interest.[106]

Labor has proposed regulations that would allow a primary service provider to develop and maintain the computer model that renders advice to participants if, among other things, the model has been certified by an independent financial expert and undergoes annual audits. Therefore, unlike the direct service or SunAmerica arrangements, where an independent advice provider is the creator of a computer model that renders advice to participants, the PPA computer model arrangement bypasses the independent advice provider and allows the primary service provider to create the computer model that renders advice to participants. In addition to permitting the use of the computer modeling advice arrangement, the PPA also permits a level fee advice arrangement, which allows a provider who may otherwise have a conflict of interest—such as a provider whose proprietary funds are part of a plan's investment lineup—to furnish investment advice to participants. Specifically, Labor's proposed regulations specify that a provider may furnish advice to participants if the provider's fees do not vary depending on participants' investment decisions. A Labor publication indicates that the level fee requirement applies to the service providers' representatives and their employers, but not their affiliates.[107]

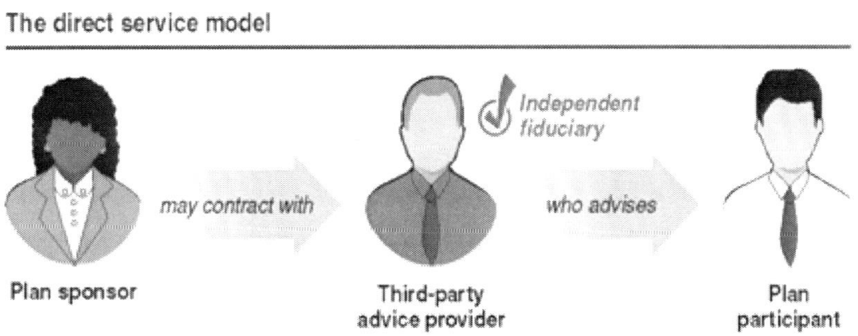

Source: GAO analysis of information from industry practitioners.

Figure 7. The Direct Service Model Advice Arrangement.

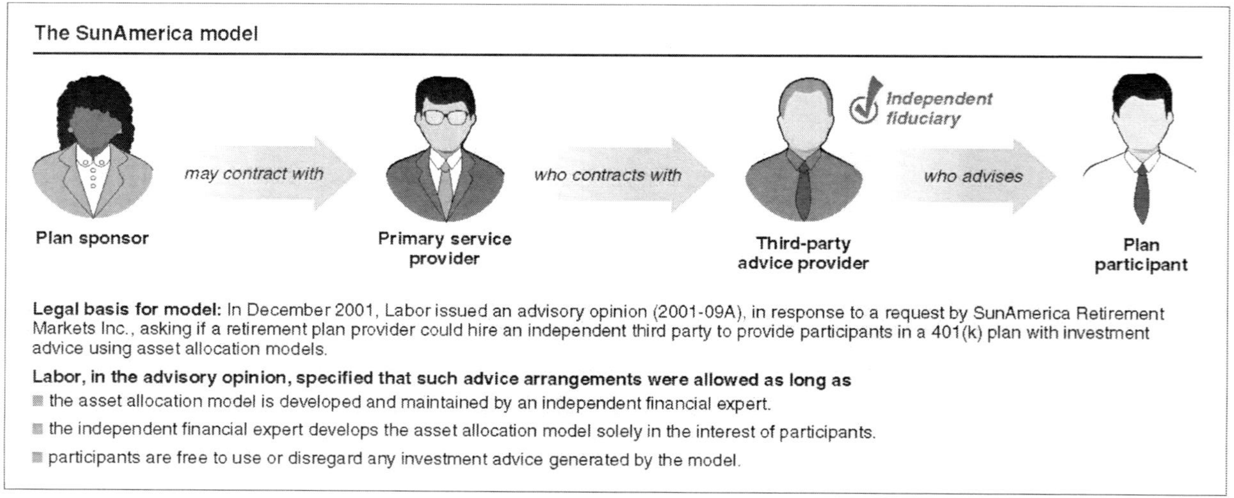

GAO analysis of information from industry practitioners and Labor's advisory opinion.

Figure 8. The SunAmerica Advice Arrangement.

The PPA computer model

Legal basis for model: The Pension Protection Act (PPA) of 2006 provided two eligible investment advice arrangements (EIAAs), in the form of statutory exemptions from ERISA's prohibited transaction rules, for fiduciaries who might otherwise have conflicts of interests when rendering investment advice

- **The PPA computer-model arrangement** allows advice to be provided to participants or beneficiaries using a computer model that, among other things, is certified by an eligible investment expert and audited annually by an independent auditor.
- **The PPA fee-leveling arrangement** allows advice to be provided to participants or beneficiaries by an adviser whose compensation does not vary depending on the basis of any investment option selected by plan participants or beneficiaries. Labor has stated that such requirement do not extend to fiduciaries' affiliates.

PPA provisions set forth compliance requirements for both of these arrangements. In addition, Labor is finalizing proposed regulations pursuant to the PPA to outline additional technical requirements for PPA EIAAs (75 Fed. Reg. 9360-70 (March 2, 2010)).

GAO analysis of information from industry practitioners and Labor's proposed regulation.

Figure 9. The PPA Computer Model Advice Arrangement.

End Notes

[1] A plan sponsor, often the employer offering a 401(k) plan, hires companies to provide a number of services necessary to operate a plan. Services can include fund management (i.e., selecting and managing the securities included in a mutual fund), consulting and investment advice (i.e., selecting vendors for investment options or other services, such as record keeping), record keeping (i.e., tracking individual account contributions), custodial or trustee services for plan assets (i.e., hold the plan assets in a bank), and telephone or Web-based customer services for participants.

[2] GAO, *Private Pensions: Changes Needed to Provide 401(k) Plan Participants and the Department of Labor Better Information on Fees,* GAO-07-21 (Washington, D.C.: Nov. 16, 2006).

[3] U.S. Bureau of Labor Statistics. *National Compensation Survey of Employee Benefits in the United States, March 2009*. Percentages can be attributed to the overall private industry workforce, not just those of private industry employees with access to defined contribution plans.

[4] See Investment Company Institute, FAQs & Resource Centers: "Frequently Asked Questions about 401(k) Plans," at http://www.ici.org/faqs/faqs_401k. A worker that actively participated in a 401(k) plan may participate in more than one DC plan and also might participate in a DB plan in addition to his or her 401(k) plan.

[5] See Alicia H. Munnell et al., *Investment Returns: Defined Benefit vs. 401(k) Plans.* (Chestnut Hill, Mass. 2006); Watson Wyatt, "Defined Benefit vs. 401(k0 Plans: Investment Returns for 2003-2006," at http://www.watsonwyatt.com/us/pubs/insider/showarticle.asp? ArticleID =19148; and Waring and Siegal, "Wake Up and Smell the Coffee! DC Plans Aren't Working: Here's How to Fix Them," *Journal of Investing* (Winter 2007).

[6] See, e.g., Annamaria Lusardi and O. S. Mitchell, Working Paper: "Financial Literacy and Planning: Implications for Retirement Wellbeing," University of Pennsylvania, Wharton School of Business, Pension Research Council (October 2006); Annamaria Lusardi and O. S. Mitchell, "Baby Boomer Retirement Security: The Roles of Planning, Financial Literacy, and Housing Wealth," 54 J, *Monetary Economics* 205, 205-24 (2007); Annamaria Lusardi, "Household Savings Behavior: The Role of Financial Literacy, Information, and Financial Education Programs," *Policymaking Insights from Behavioral Economics* (Dartmouth College and NBER 2008); A. Hung, et al., Working Paper: "Building Up, Spending Down: Financial Literacy, Retirement Savings Management, and Decumulation," RAND Corporation (2009); "Bridging the Gap Between Employers' and Workers' Understanding of 401(k) Fees," TransAmerica Center for Retirement Studies (July 2010).

[7] Lusardi, "Household Savings Behavior: The Role of Financial Literacy, Information, and Financial Education Programs," 2.

[8] TransAmerica Center for Retirement Studies, "Bridging the Gap Between Employers' and Workers' Understanding of 401(k) Fees," 10.

[9] 29 C.F.R. § 2509.96-1(d).

[10] SEC Office of Compliance Inspections and Examinations, *Staff Report Concerning Examinations of Select Pension Consultants* (Washington, D.C.: May 16, 2005).

[11] GAO, *Defined Benefit Pensions: Conflicts of Interest Involving High Risk or Terminated Plans Pose Enforcement Challenges*, GAO-07-703 (Washington, D.C.: June 28, 2007).

[12] According to the SEC report, the pension consultants examined represented a cross section of the pension consultant community and varied in size (measured in terms of the number and size of their pension plan clients) and the type of products and services they offered. About half of the pension consultants examined were among the largest pension consulting service providers, measured in terms of the assets of the plans they advise. The remainder of the sample consisted of medium and smaller consultants. Since the consultants were not selected randomly, this sample cannot be generalized to the population of pension

consultants. See, also GAO-07-703. GAO worked with SEC to obtain data to conduct a statistical analysis of rates of return associated with the consultants examined in SEC's study, including the 13 consultants identified by the SEC as having undisclosed conflicts of interest.

[13] In addition, the law states that a person acts as a fiduciary when he or she exercises any discretionary control or authority over plan management or any authority or control over plan assets, or has any discretionary authority or responsibility in the administration of a plan. 29 U.S.C. § 1002(21)(A).

[14] On October 22, 2010, EBSA proposed regulations that would eliminate the five-part test described here. These regulations, which would encompass certain advisory relationships not currently covered under the five-part test, have not been finalized, and as a result, the five-part test was in effect when our work was conducted and the regulations are still in effect as of the issuance date of this report. Definition of the Term "Fiduciary," 75 Fed. Reg. 65,263 (October 22, 2010)(to be codified at 29 C.F.R. pt. 2510).

[15] 29 C.F.R § 2510.3-21(c).

[16] ERISA's prudent man standard of care is articulated by the requirement that a fiduciary shall discharge his duties with respect to a plan solely in the interest of the participants and beneficiaries and for the exclusive purpose of providing benefits to participants and their beneficiaries and defraying reasonable expenses of administering the plan. In addition, the fiduciary is required to act with the care, skill, prudence, and diligence under the circumstances then prevailing that a prudent man acting in a like capacity and familiar with such matters would use in the conduct of an enterprise of a like character and with like aims. Furthermore, the fiduciary is to diversify the investments of the plan so as to minimize the risk of large losses, unless under the circumstances it is clearly not prudent to do so, and act in accordance with the documents and instruments governing the plan insofar as such documents and instruments are consistent with the provisions of Title I and Title IV of ERISA. 29 U.S.C. § 1104(a)(1).

[17] 29 U.S.C. § 1106. There are two main categories of prohibited transactions: (1) transactions between a plan and a party in interest and (2) fiduciary self-dealing. ERISA also provides, however, a number of detailed exemptions to these prohibitions and permits Labor to establish administrative exemptions as well. 29 U.S.C. § 1108.

[18] Under self-dealing prohibited transaction rules, fiduciaries are prohibited from (1) dealing with plan assets for his or her own interest or for his or her own account, (2) acting adverse to the plan in a transaction involving the plan, and (3) receiving consideration from a party dealing with the plan in a transaction involving plan assets. 29 U.S.C. § 1106(b).

[19] The preamble to the interim final regulations of July 16, 2010 under 29 C.F.R. § 2550.408b-2 provide that "[t]he Department notes, however, that…ERISA § 404(a) continues to obligate fiduciaries to obtain and consider information relating to the cost of plan services and potential conflicts of interest presented by such service arrangements." Reasonable Contract or Arrangement Under Section 408(b)(2)—Fee Disclosure; Interim Final Rule, 75 Fed. Reg. 41,600 (July 16, 2010) (to be codified at 29 C.F.R. pt. 2550). To provide plan sponsors and other fiduciaries with sufficient information to determine that plan expenses are reasonable and identify potential conflicts of interest, EBSA issued interim final regulations on July 16, 2010, that require service providers to disclose direct and indirect compensation to plan fiduciaries. 29 C.F.R. § 2550.408(b)(2) (2010).

[20] 29 U.S.C. § 1109.

[21] *Harris Trust & Savings Bank v. Salomon Smith Barney, Inc.*, 530 U.S. 238 (2000).

[22] 15 U.S.C. §§ 80b-1 et seq. Under current law, most investment advisers must have a minimum of $25 million in assets under management in order to register with SEC. However, current rules under the Advisers Act require pension consultants to plans having an aggregate value of at least $50 million to register with the commission (Rule 203A-2(b)). The Dodd-Frank Wall Street Reform and Consumer Protection Act, Pub. L. No. 111-203, § 410, 124 Stat. 1376, 1576 (2010), raised the threshold requirement for SEC registration to $100 million for

most investment advisers, and SEC has proposed to raise the threshold for pension consultants to $200 million (in plan assets). 75 Fed. Reg. 7,7052 (Dec. 10, 2010).

[23] Investment advisers use Form ADV under the Advisers Act to register with SEC or state securities authorities or to amend those registrations. SEC adopted amendments to Form ADV that were effective October 12, 2010, requiring a narrative brochure written in plain English. Part 1 of Form ADV provides regulators with information necessary to process registration and manage their regulatory and examination programs. See Amendments to Form ADV, 75 Fed. Reg. 49,234 (August 12, 2010) (to be codified at 17 C.F.R. pt. 275 and 279).

[24] 15 U.S.C. §§ 78a et seq. Broker-dealers are regulated by FINRA and by SEC under the federal securities laws and FINRA rules.

[25] The major securities industry self-regulatory organizations (SRO), such as FINRA, impose suitability rules that members must follow. For example, under National Association of Securities Dealers (NASD) Conduct Rule 2310, a FINRA member making an investment recommendation to a customer must have grounds for believing that the recommendation is suitable for that customer's financial situation and needs. In August 2010, FINRA proposed new consolidated rules governing the suitability obligations and know-your-customer obligations of its members. The new rules retain the core features of the current rules, while modifying both rules to strengthen and clarify them. On November 17, 2010, SEC approved the rule changes with slight modifications. See Securities Exchange Act Release No. 63325. 75 Fed. Reg. 71,479 (Nov. 23, 2010). The new rules are effective on October 7, 2011.

[26] See, e.g., *De Kwiatkowski v. Bear, Stearns & Co.*, 306 F.3d 1293, 1302 (2d Cir. 2002) (broker-dealer "is obliged to give honest and complete information when recommending a purchase or sale"); *Vucinich v. Paine, Webber, Jackson & Curtis, Inc.*, 803 F.2d 454, 459-61 (9th Cir. 1986) (vacating directed verdict for broker-dealer where evidence showed broker-dealer may have violated Exchange Act by failing to disclose material facts relating to risk to his unsophisticated customer and may effectively have exercised control over account); *SEC v. R.A. Holman & Co.*, 366 F.2d 456, 458 (2d Cir. 1966) (salespersons failed to disclose that company had significant losses).

[27] See, e.g., *Chasins v. Smith, Barney & Co.*, 438 F.2d 1167, 1172 (2d Cir. 1970); *SEC v. Hasho*, 784 F. Supp. 1059, 1110 (S.D.N.Y. 1992); *In re Richmark Capital Corp.*, Exch. Act Release No. 48758 (Nov. 7, 2003) (SEC opinion) ("When a securities dealer recommends stock to a customer, it is not only obligated to avoid affirmative misstatements, but also must disclose material adverse facts of which it is aware. That includes disclosure of 'adverse interests' such as 'economic self interest' that could have influenced its recommendation.")(citations omitted).

[28] Letter from Marc Menchel, Executive Vice President and General Counsel, FINRA, to Elizabeth M. Murphy, Secretary, SEC 4 (Aug. 25, 2010), available at http://www.finra.org/web/groups/industry/@ip/@reg/@guide/documents/industry/p121983.pdf . See, also, GAO, *Consumer Finance: Regulatory Coverage Generally Exists for Financial Planners, but Consumer Protection Issues Remain*, GAO-11-235 (Washington, D.C.: January 2011).

[29] SEC, *Study on Investment Advisers and Broker-Dealers* (Washington, D.C.: January 2011).

[30] Pub. L. No. 111-203, § 913, 124 Stat. 1376, 1824 (2010). A retail customer is defined as a natural person, or the legal representative of a natural person, who receives personalized investment advice from a broker, dealer, or investment adviser and uses the advice primarily for personal, family, or household purposes.

[31] SEC, *Study on Investment Advisers and Broker-Dealers* (Washington, D.C.: January 2011). Dodd-Frank requires that any rules that SEC proposes under the uniform fiduciary standard would be no less stringent than the standard applicable to investment advisers under section 206(1) and (2) of the Advisers Act when providing personalized investment advice about securities.

[32] As noted by the 2007 ERISA Advisory Council's Working Group on Fiduciary Responsibilities and Revenue Sharing Practices, "revenue sharing" is a broad term that has

a variety of interpretations by industry stakeholders. For example, in the context of investment companies, revenue sharing generally refers to payments by a company's investment adviser, typically to a broker-dealer or other party distributing the company's shares. See SEC, Mutual Fund Distribution Fees; Confirmations, 75 Fed. Reg. 47,064 (August 4, 2010). For purposes of our report, we consider revenue sharing to be payments made from one service provider to another in connection with services provided to the plan. In its report, the Working Group recommended that Labor develop definitions of revenue sharing-related terms designed to assist benefit plan sponsors, fiduciaries, service providers, and participants. To date Labor has not acted on this recommendation.

[33] GAO, *Private Pensions: Conflicts of Interest Can Affect Defined Benefit and Defined Contribution Plans*, GAO-09-503T (Washington, D.C.: Mar. 24, 2009). In the Frost Advisory Opinion 97-15A, regarding ERISA section 406(b)(1) and (3), Labor specifies that revenue-sharing payments should be fully disclosed to the plan and used to offset expenses on a dollar-for-dollar basis or else rebated to the plan if the revenue-sharing payments are made to benefit the fiduciary with discretion over the plan or participant investment or a person in whom the fiduciary would have an interest.

[34] Many mutual funds offer different classes of shares. While each share class in a fund invests in the same pool of securities, the share classes can vary in the shareholder services and fees charged. Consequently, different share classes of the same fund can have different net returns.

[35] *In the Matter of Callan Associates*, Order Instituting Administrative And Cease-And-Desist Proceedings, Advisers Act Release No. 2650 (September 19, 2007). Following the SEC investigation, the service provider revised its disclosures to include the compensation contingent from the brokerage firm. In addition, SEC ordered the respondent to cease and desist from committing or causing any violations and any future violations of section 207 of the Advisers Act.

[36] Under a safe harbor provision in section 28(e) of the Securities Exchange Act of 1934, advisers are permitted to pay more than the lowest available commission rate for security transactions in return for research and brokerage services and not be in breach of their fiduciary duty. 15 U.S.C. § 78bb(e). In order to be protected against a claim of breach of fiduciary duty under this safe harbor provision, the adviser must make a good faith determination that the amount of commission paid is reasonable in relation to the value of the brokerage and research services provided by the broker-dealer.

[37] Commission revenues can be used to pay fees of other service providers through a directed brokerage arrangement, also referred to as "commission recapture." In a directed brokerage arrangement, the plan directs the fund manager to use a specified broker-dealer, which will then rebate all or a portion of the commission revenues to the plan or pay the fees of another service provider, such as the investment adviser.

[38] See SEC, *Staff Report Concerning Examinations of Select Pension Consultants* (Washington, D.C.: May 16, 2005), 4. SEC officials told us the issues identified in their review of pension consultants were resolved through remediation.

[39] As mentioned previously, on October 22, 2010, EBSA published proposed regulations that would eliminate the current five-part test and establish a new definition to be used to determine whether a service provider is a fiduciary. In the preamble to the proposed regulations, EBSA acknowledge that the five-part test, which has not been updated since its promulgation in 1975, "significantly narrows" the plain language of the statutory definition of fiduciary. 75 Fed. Reg. 65,263, 65,264.

[40] U.S. Department of Labor, Office of Inspector General, *EBSA Needs to Do More to Protect Retirement Plan Assets from Conflicts of Interest*, Report No. 09-10-001-12-121, September 30, 2010.

[41] Information from EBSA generally confirms that this practice is occurring to some degree. Specifically, EBSA has acknowledged that its recent enforcement activities indicate that there are a variety of circumstances, outside those described in the five-part test, under

which plan fiduciaries seek out impartial assistance and expertise of persons such as consultants and other advisers for advice on investment-related matters. According to EBSA, these persons significantly influence the decisions of plan fiduciaries and have a considerable impact on investments; however, if these advisers are not fiduciaries under ERISA (as they are often not under the current five-part test), they often operate with conflicts of interest that they do not disclose to plan fiduciaries who expect impartiality. EBSA notes further that "the current test . . . makes it easy for consultants to structure their actions to avoid fiduciary status." 75 Fed. Reg. 65,263, 65,265, 65,271.

[42] 15 U.S.C. § 80b-1 et seq., Rule 204-3, and Form ADV.

[43] However, Labor issued interim final regulation due to take effect in July 2011 that will require certain service providers to disclose information to assist plan fiduciaries in assessing the reasonableness of contracts or arrangements, including the reasonableness of the service providers' compensation and potential conflicts of interest, that may affect the service providers' performance. 75 Fed. Reg. 41,600.

[44] 29 U.S.C. § 1102(a) and GAO, *Private Pensions: Fulfilling Fiduciary Obligations Can Present Challenges for 401(k) Plan Sponsors*, GAO-08-774 (Washington, D.C.: July 16, 2008).

[45] A service provider may be a fiduciary for purposes of some services it provides to a plan, but not others. For example, a service provider may be an ERISA fiduciary by virtue of having responsibility for the administration of a plan, but the same company may not be an ERISA fiduciary when providing investment assistance that does not meet the five-part test.

[46] EBSA's interim final regulations scheduled to take effect in July 2011 require certain service providers to disclose to plan sponsors whether they reasonably expect to provide services as a fiduciary under their contract or arrangement with the plan. See proposed 29 C.F.R. § 2550.408b-2(c)(1)(iv)(B), 75 Fed. Reg. 41,600, 41,635.

[47] GAO 08-774.

[48] The preamble to EBSA's proposed regulations of October 22, 2010, notes that the five-part test applies even to persons who represent themselves to the plan as fiduciaries in rendering advice. The preamble explains that a consultant could hold itself out as a plan fiduciary in a written contract with the plan, render investment advice for a fee, and still evade fiduciary status by structuring its activities to avoid meeting some element of the five-part test. 75 Fed. Reg. 65,263, 65,271.

[49] Broker-dealers are subject to a system of regulations. They generally are required to make recommendations that are consistent with the interests of their customers and generally must disclose material conflicts of interest to their customers when making recommendations. As noted above, Dodd-Frank gives SEC the authority to issue regulations harmonizing the standards of conduct required of investment advisers and broker-dealers when providing personalized investment advice about securities to retail clients and other such customers as SEC may provide by rule. If SEC promulgates such rules, broker-dealers and investment advisers would be required to act in the best interests of their customers without regard to their own financial or other interests, and disclose material conflicts of interest. The rules shall also provide that such standard of conduct shall be no less stringent than the standard applicable to investment advisers under Sections 206(1) and (2) of the Advisers Act.

[50] 75 Fed. Reg. 41,600, 41,603.

[51] Frost Advisory Opinion 97-15A and ERISA § 406(b)(3). In addition, Labor proposed interim final regulations in July 2010 to require service providers report sources of direct and indirect compensation to plan sponsors. These regulations are scheduled to become effective in July 2011.

[52] SEC and Labor, *Selecting and Monitoring Pension Consultants: Tips for Plan Fiduciaries*, http://www.sec.gov/investor/pubs/sponsortips.htm, June 2005.

[53] In one case, the 401(k) plan sponsor was found to have breached its fiduciary duty of prudence by choosing to offer investments in the retail share class rather than the institutional share class of certain funds, which engaged in revenue sharing. *Tibble v. Edison Int'l*, 2010 WL 2757153 (C.D. Cal. July 8, 2010).

[54] GAO-07-703. In this report on DB plans, we found lower annual rates of return for ongoing plans associated with pension consultants who had failed to disclose significant conflicts of interest, with lower rates generally ranging from a statistically significant 1.2 to 1.3 percentage points over the 2000 to 2004 period. Although this negative association between the presence of a conflict of interest and investment returns is consistent with what industry experts told us, limitations of this analysis did not allow us to establish causality.

[55] Department of Labor, *A Look at 401(k) Plan Fees*, http://www.dol.gov/ebsa/publications/401k_employee.html . GAO 07-21. Janet Rubenstein and Jeff Marzinsky, *A 401(k) Plan that Works—the "Bundled Unbundled" Solution*, Milliman White Paper, February 21, 2007. Over a 35-year time horizon, EBSA estimates that a 1 percentage point increase in fees reduces final savings by 28 percent. Over a 20-year time horizon, GAO estimates that a 1 percentage point increase in fees reduces final savings by 17 percent. Over a 40-year time horizon, Rubenstein and Marzinsky estimate that a 1 percentage point increase in fees reduces final savings by 26 percent. In addition, a study by the Center for Retirement Research estimates that a 0.7 percentage point fee reduces final savings by more than 12.5 percent over a 30-year time horizon. See Richard W. Kopcke, Francis M. Vitagliano, and Zhenya S. Karamcheva, *Reducing Costs of 401(k) Plans with ETFs and Commingled Trusts*, Center for Retirement Research at Boston College, July 2010.

[56] The various formats used for furnishing investment education and advice are described in appendix II. The various types of computer models used to dispense investment advice are described in appendix III.

[57] 29 U.S.C. §§ 1002(21)(A)(ii). See also 29 C.F.R. § 2509.96-1 concerning constraints involving participant education.

[58] 29 C.F.R. § 2509.96-1(d)(3)(iii).

[59] A service provider who may otherwise have a conflict of interest may furnish investment advice using either the SunAmerica arrangement (EBSA Advisory Opinion 2001-09A), which requires a provider to contract with an independent advice provider to furnish advice, or the PPA computer model arrangement, which allows a provider to furnish advice in-house if the provider can meet specific compliance requirements See appendix III for more information on the advice arrangements.

[60] The PPA arrangement, which allows the fiduciary adviser to design the computer model, requires the model to undergo annual audits. By contrast, the SunAmerica arrangement relies upon an independent financial expert to develop the computer model and does not require the model to undergo annual audits.

[61] See, e.g., Hewitt Associates. *Trends and Experience in 401(k) Plans*. (Hewitt Associates LLC, 2009); Hewitt Associates, *Help in Defined Contribution Plans: Is It Working and for Whom?* (Hewitt Associates LLC, 2010); Annamaria Lusardi, "Household Savings Behavior: The Role of Literacy, Information, and Financial Education Programs." (Dartmouth College and NBER 2008).

[62] Because of methodological limitations associated with the polls with SHRM and SPARK, results from these polls represent only the views of the poll respondents. Please see appendix I for further details regarding our methodology.

[63] A former employee with a retirement plan account balance of $5,000 or more may keep funds in the existing plan after leaving a job. See 29 U.S.C. § 1053(e)(1) and 26 U.S.C. § 411(a)(11)(A).

[64] From 1998 to 2007, rollovers into IRAs constituted $2.25 trillion of the $2.69 trillion in total funds flowing into IRAs. As of year end 2009, an estimated $4.2 trillion of total U.S. retirement assets was held in IRAs, while $4.1 trillion was held in DC plans (including 401(k)s). See Investment Company Institute, "The U.S. Retirement Market, 2009," *Research Fundamentals*, Vol. 19, No. 3, 3 (May 2010).

[65] The 2004 SIPP surveyed sampled U.S. households (with sample sizes ranging from approximately 14,000 to 36,700 households) in different waves over a 2.5-year period, with interviews lasting into 2006. About 7 million (7,055,207) survey respondents received a

lump-sum distribution of their plan funds from a previous employer. Of these, about 69 percent—or 4,868,093 survey respondents—rolled over their funds into an IRA. See United States Department of Commerce. Bureau of the Census, 2005-11-02, "Survey of Income and Program Participation (SIPP) [2004 Panel, Wave 7].

[66] EBSA Advisory Opinion 2005-23A (December 7, 2005).

[67] In its preamble to the proposed new definition of fiduciary, the department noted that as a general matter, a recommendation to a plan participant to take an otherwise permissible distribution does not constitute investment advice within the meaning of the current regulation, when that advice is combined with a recommendation as to how the distribution should be invested. However, the department further notes that concerns have been expressed that as a result of that position, plan participants may not be adequately protected from advisers who provide distribution recommendations that subordinate participants' interests to the advisers' own interests. The department then solicited comments on whether and to what extent the final regulation should define the provision of investment advice to encompass recommendations related to taking a plan distribution. 75 Fed. Reg. 65,263, 65,266.

[68] GAO, *Retirement Savings: Better Information and Sponsor Guidance Could Improve Oversight and Reduce Fees for Participants,* GAO-09-641 (Washington, D.C.: Sept. 4, 2009).

[69] Investment Advice—Participants and Beneficiaries, 75 Fed. Reg. 9,360 (March 2, 2010) (to be codified at 29 C.F.R. pt. 2550).

[70] Notice to Participants of Consequences of Failing to Defer Receipt of Qualified Retirement Plan Distributions; Expansion of Applicable Election Period for Notices, 73 Fed. Reg. 59,575 (October 9, 2008) (to be codified at 26 C.F.R. pt. 1). Section 1102(b)(1) of the Pension Protection Act of 2006 instructs the Secretary of the Treasury to provide a description to participants of the consequences of taking a distribution.

[71] This applies to EBSA's civil investigations. For EBSA's criminal investigations, however, the subject of the investigation need not be an ERISA fiduciary because an allegation of fraud is sufficient to trigger EBSA's jurisdiction.

[72] GAO-07-703 .

[73] 29 C.F.R. § 2510.3-21.

[74] As we reported in 2007, given EBSA's other enforcement responsibilities, EBSA officials told us that they concentrate on a relatively small number of these conflict of interest cases because they are so complex. GAO-07-703.

[75] However, the department's new proposal to modify the definition of fiduciary should provide some relief from the problems previously associated with the five-part test. In its proposed rulemaking, EBSA explained that it is appropriate to update the "investment advice" definition to better ensure that persons, in fact, providing investment advice to plan fiduciaries and/or plan participants and beneficiaries are subject to ERISA's standards of fiduciary conduct. 75 Fed. Reg. 65,263, 65,265.

[76] While only 16 CAP cases have been closed, 7 of the open CAP cases involve an ongoing criminal investigation or an investigation related to a currently open ongoing criminal investigation.

[77] SEC, Office of Compliance Inspections and Examinations, *Staff Report Concerning Examinations of Select Pension Consultants* (Washington, D.C.: May 16, 2005).

[78] Labor OIG-Office of Audit, *EBSA Needs To Do More To Protect Retirement Plan Assets From Conflicts Of Interest, 09-10-001-12-121* (Washington, D.C.: Sept. 30, 2010). There is a difference between fiduciary requirements specified by ERISA and requirements specified by the Advisers Act. Because of this difference, EBSA and SEC were able to take different measures to resolve the conflicts of interest found for these 13 consultants. In accordance with the Advisers Act, the problems identified by SEC were resolved through remediation and SEC enforcement efforts. As a result, SEC reported that many of these consultants took corrective action—changed policies and procedures to insulate their advisory activities from

other activities, improved disclosure of conflicts of interest, and prevented conflicts of interest in certain respects.

[79] GAO, *Employee Benefits Security Administration: Enforcement Improvements Made but Additional Actions Could Further Enhance Pension Plan Oversight*, GAO-07-22 (Washington, D.C.: Jan. 18, 2007). As we previously reported, a compliance examination program, in part, is designed to establish a presence by regularly reviewing entities' operations, thereby likely creating a deterrent to noncompliance. Implementing such routine compliance examinations may displace some resources currently dedicated to enforcement efforts, but would provide an evidence-driven method for evaluating the success of those enforcement efforts.

[80] Advisory Opinion 2001-09A (2001).

[81] 75 Fed. Reg. 9,360.

[82] SEC, *Staff Report Concerning Examinations of Select Pension Consultants* (Washington, D.C.: May 16, 2005). According to EBSA officials, EBSA has fostered relationships with SEC at local levels to obtain future referrals.

[83] EBSA published final regulations on October 20, 2010, to improve participant fee disclosure. While these disclosures will provide information about the performance and fees of different investment options available within the plan, it does not include complete information on compensation to service providers. Fiduciary Requirements for Disclosure in Participant-Directed Individual Account Plans; Final Rule, 75 Fed. Reg. 64,910 (October 20, 2010) (codified at 29 C.F.R. § 2550.404a-5).

[84] According to EBSA, several cases have also been referred to the Office of the Solicitor General for further action.

[85] GAO-07-22 .

[86] 75 Fed. Reg. 65,263.

[87] In the preamble to the proposed regulations, EBSA acknowledges that the five-part test takes a narrow approach to fiduciary status that "sharply limits" its ability to protect plans and their participants and beneficiaries from conflicts of interest that may arise from the diverse and complex fee practices existing in today's retirement plan services market and to devise effective remedies for misconduct when it occurs. Accordingly, the new proposed regulations are intended to more broadly define the circumstances under which a person is considered a fiduciary by reason of giving investment advice to a plan or its participants. 75 Fed. Reg. 65,263, 65,271.

[88] See proposed 29 C.F.R. § 2510.3-21(c), 75 Fed. Reg. 65,263, 65,277.

[89] See proposed 29 C.F.R. § 2510.3-21(c)(2)(ii)(B), 75 Fed. Reg. 65,263, 65,277.

[90] 75 Fed. Reg. 41,600.

[91] A covered plan is a pension plan—all ERISA-governed retirement plans, including 403(b) arrangements—but does not include Simplified Employee Pension IRAs, Savings Incentive Match Plan for Employees IRAs, or IRAs.

[92] A covered service provider is a service provider that enters into an arrangement with a plan and reasonably expects to receive $1,000 or more in compensation, direct or indirect, in connection with the services described in the regulation. The interim final rule specifies that covered service providers include some service providers acting as ERISA fiduciaries and some service providers who may not be ERISA fiduciaries.

[93] ERISA § 408(b)(2) and Code § 4975(d)(2) state that services by providers are prohibited unless (1) the contract or arrangement is reasonable, (2) the services are necessary for the plan, and (3) no more than reasonable compensation is paid. The regulations provide specific definitions for plans and service providers that are covered under the revised section 408(b)(2).

[94] See proposed 29 C.F.R. § 2550.408b-2(c)(1)(iv)(B), 75 Fed. Reg. 41,600, 41,635.

[95] EBSA notes that this change to the regulations would permit its investigators and attorneys to focus their efforts on the adviser's conduct rather than meeting the evidentiary requirements to prove all elements of the current five-part test are satisfied and would enhance its ability

to redress service provider abuses that currently exist in the market. 75 Fed. Reg. 65,263, 65,272.

[96] These disclosures must be made in writing and in advance of the date the arrangement is entered into, and extended or renewed, and any changes to this information must be disclosed as soon as is practicable, but not later than 60 days from the date on which the service provider is informed of the changes.

[97] In the preamble to the interim final regulations, EBSA noted that it is persuaded that plan fiduciaries may benefit from increased uniformity in the way that information is presented to them. However, EBSA explained that it does not want to unnecessarily increase the cost and burden for service providers to furnish information, especially because such costs may be passed along to plan participants and beneficiaries, unless it is clear that the benefit to fiduciaries outweighs such costs and burdens. EBSA requested comments addressing (1) the likely cost and burden to service providers of complying with a requirement that information be disclosed in a particular format, (2) the anticipated benefits to plan fiduciaries of including a summary disclosure statement, and (3) how to most effectively construct the requirement for a summary disclosure statement to ensure both its feasibility and its usefulness. The comment period closed on August 30, 2010, and the department has not yet issued final regulations. 75 Fed. Reg. 41,600, 41,607.

[98] The interim final regulations only apply to employer-sponsored plans under ERISA, not to IRAs.

[99] 75 Fed. Reg. 64,910 (October 20, 2010).

[100] Under the proposal, two eligible investment arrangements are available in the form of statutory exemptions from the prohibited transaction rules. These rules would normally prohibit a fiduciary who might otherwise be a party in interest from furnishing investment advice to the plan or its participants. These two arrangements are (1) a computer model arrangement, where advice is rendered that, among other requirements, must be certified by an eligible investment expert and audited annually by an independent auditor, and (2) advice may be rendered by an adviser whose compensation does not vary based on the option selected by the plan participant. 75 Fed. Reg. 9,360.

[101] See, e.g., Hewitt Associates. *Trends and Experience in 401(k) Plans*. (Hewitt Associates LLC, 2009); Hewitt Associates, *Help in Defined Contribution Plans: Is It Working and for Whom?* (Hewitt Associates LLC, 2010); Annamaria Lusardi, "Household Savings Behavior: The Role of Literacy, Information, and Financial Education Programs." (Dartmouth College and NBER 2008).

[102] Because of methodological limitations associated with the polls with SHRM and SPARK, results from these polls represent only the views of the poll respondents. Please see appendix I for further details regarding our methodology.

[103] The 52nd annual survey of profit-sharing and 401(k) plans for 2008 by PSCA. The survey was published in 2009, but reflects 2008 plan experience. The survey was based on results from 908 plans—28 profit-sharing plans, 607 401(k) plans, and 273 combination profit-sharing and 401(k) plans— with 7.4 million participants.

[104] Among plans that participated in PSCA's annual survey in 2008, 58 percent of plans used one-on-one counseling sessions to deliver advice, 44 percent of plans used Internet providers to deliver advice, and 31.9 percent of plans used telephone hotlines to deliver advice.

[105] Among plans that participated in PSCA's annual survey in 2008, 82.7 percent of plans with fewer than 50 participants use one-on-one counseling sessions to deliver advice, while 73.9 percent of larger plans with 5,000-plus participants use Internet providers to deliver advice.

[106] EBSA officials anticipate finalizing proposed regulations for the PPA sometime during May 2011.

[107] Department of Labor, Field Assistance Bulletin No. 2007-01 (February 2, 2007).

INDEX

A

abuse, 28, 103
access, 25, 32, 98, 105, 114
accessibility, 47
accounting, 33, 34, 38, 46
adjustment, 4, 37
administrators, 18
adverse effects, 67
age, 4, 7, 8, 10, 11, 14, 15, 18, 24, 25, 26, 38, 84
agencies, 91, 92
annual rate, 119
annuities, ix, 9, 22, 41, 42, 54
assessment, 45
assets, ix, 3, 9, 10, 11, 18, 22, 23, 24, 26, 27, 28, 29, 32, 37, 41, 42, 43, 45, 49, 52, 54, 58, 59, 60, 61, 64, 67, 68, 71, 72, 75, 76, 86, 90, 91, 95, 100, 107, 114, 115, 119
audit(s), 60, 81, 98, 108, 111, 119
authority(s), 63, 68, 90, 94, 103, 115, 116, 118
aversion, 46

B

ban, 48
bankers, 25
banks, 5
basis points, 30, 31, 32, 33, 34, 37, 38, 57, 67
beneficiaries, 10, 63, 64, 68, 83, 84, 99, 101, 115, 120, 121, 122
benefits, 4, 19, 45, 60, 63, 115, 122
beverages, 5
bias, 36, 58, 98
board members, 106
bonds, ix, 22, 38, 54
business cycle, 38
businesses, 62, 75, 76

C

call centers, 61
CAP, 57, 90, 91, 120
cash, 36, 88, 107
causality, 119
Census, 86, 106, 120
CFR, 19
challenges, 46, 47, 61, 81, 99, 100
charities, 8
classes, 27, 56, 63, 67, 72, 81, 84, 117
clients, ix, 22, 25, 26, 27, 31, 32, 34, 35, 36, 47, 48, 61, 65, 68, 69, 71, 73, 76, 78, 81, 114, 118
collateral, 5
combined effect, 38
communication, 105
community(s), 16, 114

competing interests, 58
complexity, 25, 81, 99
compliance, 84, 91, 92, 105, 119, 121
composition, 23
comprehension, 47
computation, 41
computer, 61, 82, 83, 84, 98, 109, 110, 111, 119, 122
computing, 7, 13
conflict, 26, 30, 31, 34, 37, 38, 41, 42, 43, 56, 58, 66, 67, 68, 70, 71, 72, 73, 75, 76, 77, 78, 81, 82, 83, 90, 91, 98, 99, 101, 110, 111, 119, 120
conflict of interest, 26, 56, 58, 66, 67, 68, 70, 71, 72, 73, 75, 76, 77, 78, 81, 82, 83, 90, 91, 98, 99, 101, 110, 111, 119, 120
Congress, vii, 1, 8, 16, 17, 18, 19, 104
congressional requests, 102
consulting, 104, 114
Consumer Price Index, 4
consumer protection, 28, 47
consumers, 26, 27, 46
contribution limits, viii, 2, 3, 7, 13
contribution plan, viii, 16, 21, 23, 25, 54, 86, 105, 107, 114
coordination, 85, 100, 105, 109
cost, vii, 4, 22, 23, 30, 31, 38, 41, 42, 43, 48, 49, 64, 67, 81, 95, 102, 115, 122
cost-benefit analysis, 102
counseling, 110, 122
covering, 71
criminal investigations, 120
customer service, 38, 114
customers, 26, 43, 65, 66, 68, 69, 118

D

database, 107
deduction, 6, 7
defined benefit pension, 6
Department of Commerce, 120
Department of Labor, vii, ix, 55, 59, 102, 104, 114, 119, 122
Department of the Treasury, 56, 100, 104
deposits, 9
disability, 14
disaster, 8, 17, 19
disaster area, 17, 19
disclosure, 47, 48, 50, 56, 57, 60, 65, 69, 78, 87, 88, 92, 93, 94, 95, 96, 97, 99, 100, 101, 102, 103, 116, 121, 122
distribution, viii, 2, 7, 9, 10, 11, 15, 17, 18, 33, 34, 50, 72, 86, 103, 120
diversification, 35, 61
Dodd-Frank Wall Street Reform and Consumer Protection Act, 66, 115
draft, 102, 104

E

earnings, viii, 2, 4, 5, 7, 12, 14, 23, 24, 38, 43, 45, 46
economic losses, 17
economic relations, 29
economics, 29, 47
education, 46, 48, 56, 58, 61, 63, 82, 83, 85, 100, 101, 103, 105, 109, 119
educational materials, 101
eligibility requirements, viii, 2
e-mail, 106
Emergency Economic Stabilization Act, 17
empirical studies, 30, 41
employees, vii, 1, 3, 9, 18, 36, 60, 105, 114
employers, viii, 2, 5, 9, 18, 21, 25, 60, 88, 111
employer-sponsored, vii, 1, 3, 5, 6, 14, 15, 122
employment, vii, 1, 8, 24
enforcement, 57, 59, 64, 65, 71, 72, 76, 89, 90, 91, 92, 93, 94, 100, 103, 108, 117, 120, 121
enhanced service, 94
equity, 31, 33, 54, 95
estate planning, 26
European Parliament, 48, 51
European Union, 48
evidence, vii, 22, 29, 30, 33, 36, 37, 38, 41, 43, 44, 47, 49, 60, 99, 108, 116, 121
evolution, 93
examinations, 65, 73, 91, 92, 121

exchange-traded funds, ix, 22, 25
exclusion, 84, 98
execution, 69, 73
exercise, 94
expertise, 61, 80, 102, 118
exposure, 32, 38

F

fairness, 69
faith, 95, 117
families, viii, 22, 54
federal law, 59, 68, 69
Federal Reserve, 107
Federal Reserve Board, 107
financial, ix, 5, 13, 19, 22, 25, 26, 27, 28, 29, 30, 35, 36, 42, 43, 46, 47, 48, 50, 51, 54, 55, 56, 58, 59, 60, 61, 63, 66, 79, 81, 82, 83, 87, 99, 100, 101, 103, 110, 111, 116, 118, 119
financial advisers, ix, 22, 27, 30, 35, 36, 46, 47
financial decision, ix, 22, 25, 28, 36
financial institutions, 5, 13, 19
financial markets, ix, 51, 54, 55
flooding, 16, 17
floods, 3, 8
fluctuations, 38
formula, 24
fraud, 65, 120

G

GAO, ix, 28, 34, 37, 52, 55, 56, 62, 63, 69, 70, 72, 74, 76, 77, 78, 81, 84, 88, 102, 107, 108, 109, 111, 112, 113, 114, 115, 116, 117, 118, 119, 120, 121
Germany, 32, 48
growth, 2
guidance, 38, 61, 64, 83, 100
Gulf of Mexico, viii, 2, 3, 16

H

higher education, 8
honesty, 47
House, 58
House of Representatives, 58
Human Resource Management, 58, 59, 85, 105
hurricanes, viii, 2, 3, 16

I

identification, 94, 95
incidence, 106
income, vii, viii, ix, 1, 2, 4, 5, 6, 7, 8, 9, 10, 12, 13, 14, 15, 17, 18, 19, 21, 23, 25, 26, 43, 46, 55, 60, 61, 63, 85, 86, 99, 106
income tax, 4, 6, 7, 8, 9, 15
independence, 62
indexing, 3
India, 48
Individual Retirement Accounts, vii, viii, 1, 2, 18, 19, 21, 23
individuals, vii, viii, 1, 2, 3, 5, 6, 9, 12, 13, 14, 15, 16, 17, 18, 19, 22, 28, 36, 42, 47, 54, 63, 106
industry(s), 28, 29, 30, 43, 52, 56, 59, 60, 62, 66, 70, 71, 72, 73, 74, 76, 77, 78, 79, 80, 81, 83, 84, 85, 86, 91, 93, 96, 98, 99, 102, 104, 105, 106, 108, 111, 112, 113, 114, 116, 117, 119
inflation, 3, 4, 13, 38, 63
infrastructure, 43
institutions, 5
integrity, 99
intermediaries, 30, 31, 36
Internal Revenue Service, 3, 16, 57, 107
investment advisers, viii, 21, 26, 62, 65, 66, 69, 73, 78, 83, 108, 115, 116, 118
investment options, vii, ix, 25, 32, 38, 55, 56, 58, 59, 61, 67, 74, 75, 76, 78, 80, 82, 83, 84, 88, 93, 96, 98, 99, 102, 103, 110, 114, 121

investors, 27, 28, 31, 32, 33, 34, 36, 41, 45, 47, 65, 71, 72, 73
Iowa, 19
IRA, viii, 2, 3, 4, 5, 6, 7, 8, 9, 10, 11, 12, 13, 14, 15, 16, 18, 19, 22, 23, 24, 25, 28, 29, 30, 34, 37, 38, 41, 42, 43, 47, 49, 51, 54, 57, 59, 85, 86, 87, 88, 100, 103, 106, 107, 120
issues, 32, 90, 102, 117
Italy, 48

J

jurisdiction, 120
justification, 45, 48

L

landscape, viii, 21, 23
laws, 51, 59, 65, 69, 72, 76, 104, 116
laws and regulations, 59, 69
lawyers, 25
lead, 25, 32, 33, 36, 37, 38, 46, 47, 56, 58, 81
legislation, 17
life expectancy, 7, 8, 11, 15, 19, 84
lifetime, 14, 28
light, 101
literacy, 61
litigation, 71
loans, 5, 18
local government, 9
loyalty, 25, 26

M

magnitude, 32, 35, 37, 43, 81
majority, viii, 21, 23, 28, 31, 35
man, 68, 69, 115
management, 29, 36, 38, 46, 61, 64, 67, 68, 73, 114, 115
marketing, 31, 57, 71, 72, 86, 93, 100
marketplace, 28
married couples, 2
materials, 61, 63, 82, 84, 85, 109
matter, 69, 120
media, 91, 107
medical, 8, 29
medical care, 29
metals, 5
methodology, 60, 95, 106, 119, 122
mid-career, 38
mission, 103
Missouri, 19
models, 61, 63, 82, 83, 84, 98, 110, 119
modifications, 116
money market accounts, ix, 22
mortality, 96
mutual funds, ix, 5, 22, 25, 29, 30, 32, 33, 34, 35, 41, 42, 44, 46, 51, 54, 60, 72, 95, 107, 117

N

negative effects, 27
net investment, 60
Netherlands, 48
neutral, 67

O

objective criteria, 84
objectivity, 62
officials, 59, 71, 77, 89, 91, 92, 104, 105, 108, 117, 120, 121, 122
operations, 69, 121
opportunities, 46
optimism, 46
oversight, 103
overweight, 46
ownership, 10, 38

P

palladium, 18
pension plans, viii, 9, 15, 19, 21, 23, 54, 90
pensions, viii, 3, 6, 18, 21, 23, 24, 25
permission, 86

permit, 56, 72, 101, 121
plan sponsors, vii, ix, 55, 58, 59, 61, 62, 63, 64, 72, 75, 76, 77, 78, 79, 80, 81, 85, 86, 89, 90, 92, 93, 94, 96, 97, 99, 101, 102, 103, 104, 105, 108, 109, 115, 117, 118
platinum, 18
playing, 43
policy, viii, 21, 25, 48
policy issues, viii, 21, 25
policymakers, 107
population, 106, 114
portfolio, 25, 31, 32, 36, 38, 48
portfolio management, 31, 48
President, 17
principles, 65, 69
product market, 86
professionals, 26, 83, 84, 85, 98, 104, 105
profit, 24, 75, 82, 105, 110, 122
project, 57
proliferation, 25
proposed regulations, 56, 59, 84, 93, 98, 100, 101, 111, 115, 117, 118, 121, 122
protection, 28, 48, 66
psychology, 47

Q

questionnaire, 105, 109

R

rate of return, 81
recommendations, 26, 33, 36, 48, 56, 58, 62, 65, 69, 75, 76, 77, 78, 98, 100, 102, 103, 110, 118, 120
recovery, 64
reform(s), 2, 50, 66, 115
regulations, 48, 56, 57, 59, 63, 69, 76, 77, 78, 84, 87, 89, 90, 92, 93, 94, 96, 97, 99, 101, 102, 104, 105, 108, 111, 115, 117, 118, 121, 122
reimburse, 67, 71, 72
relevance, 47
reliability, 59, 108
relief, 3, 18, 120
remediation, 117, 120
requirements, viii, 2, 10, 16, 18, 48, 65, 68, 69, 83, 84, 87, 88, 92, 94, 98, 100, 102, 103, 110, 111, 119, 120, 121, 122
researchers, 31, 32, 35, 36, 107
resources, 23, 43, 50, 80, 91, 99, 102, 121
response, vii, 1, 16, 17, 83, 97, 102
restoration, 90
retail, 32, 35, 47, 48, 65, 66, 116, 118
retirement accounts, viii, 2, 54, 59, 107
retirement age, 84
retirement plan, vii, viii, 1, 5, 9, 13, 14, 15, 16, 17, 18, 21, 22, 23, 32, 33, 36, 38, 53, 54, 61, 83, 86, 88, 89, 102, 105, 107, 119, 121
retirement savings, vii, viii, 1, 2, 3, 18, 21, 22, 23, 38, 43, 49, 54, 57, 59, 61, 81, 88, 89
Retirement Savings Contribution Credit, viii, 2, 15
revenue, 26, 27, 36, 42, 54, 56, 59, 66, 67, 70, 72, 74, 75, 76, 80, 81, 95, 101, 116, 117, 118
risk(s), 24, 31, 32, 34, 35, 38, 60, 61, 63, 84, 92, 98, 115, 116
risk management, 92
risk profile, 38, 63
risk-taking, 32, 34
Rollovers, viii, 2, 9, 13, 14, 22, 51, 87
Roth IRAs, vii, viii, 1, 2, 3, 9, 11, 12, 13, 14, 15, 17, 18, 19, 28
rules, viii, 2, 3, 10, 13, 15, 18, 64, 66, 68, 69, 72, 84, 115, 116, 118, 122

S

savings, vii, viii, 1, 2, 3, 18, 21, 22, 23, 24, 26, 28, 36, 38, 42, 43, 49, 54, 57, 59, 61, 81, 83, 88, 89, 101, 119
savings account, vii, ix, 1, 22, 54
scope, 28, 103, 104, 108
Secretary of the Treasury, 102, 120
Securities Exchange Act, 65, 68, 73, 116, 117

security(s), viii, 21, 23, 64, 65, 68, 69, 72, 76, 99, 104, 114, 116, 117, 118
self-employment, 4
seminars, 61, 109
September 11, 8
services, 5, 26, 31, 43, 45, 48, 50, 61, 62, 64, 67, 68, 69, 71, 73, 75, 76, 79, 85, 86, 88, 94, 95, 96, 99, 105, 107, 114, 115, 117, 118, 121
silver, 18
small businesses, 18
Social Security, viii, 21, 23, 26
software, 61, 63
Solicitor General, 121
spin, 91
stakeholders, 117
state(s), 9, 16, 17, 62, 63, 77, 80, 82, 87, 89, 93, 103, 115, 116, 121
statistics, 107
statutes, 105
stock, 5, 36, 116
stocks and bonds, ix, 22, 38
storms, viii, 2, 8, 16, 17
structure, 56, 58, 76, 89, 118
structuring, 118
supervision, 69
Supreme Court, 19, 69

T

target, 84, 98
tax credit, viii, 2, 3, 15
tax deduction, 15
tax incentive, vii, 1
tax penalty, vii, 2, 8, 9
taxable income, vii, 2, 10, 12, 14, 17
tax-deductible, vii, 1, 2, 4, 5
tax-deferred, viii, 2
taxes, 4, 5, 9, 12, 15
tax-free, viii, 2, 3, 18
taxpayers, vii, 1, 3, 15
teams, 52
technical comments, 102, 104
technological advances, 43
telephone, 110, 114, 122
tenure, 24
time constraints, 103
time periods, 86
Title I, 64, 115
Title IV, 115
total costs, 29
trade, 35, 46, 65, 107
traits, 32
transactions, 5, 36, 47, 64, 68, 69, 73, 90, 91, 101, 104, 108, 115, 117
transparency, 47, 48
Treasury, 56, 89, 102
treatment, vii, 2, 18
turnover, 35

U

U.S. Bureau of Labor Statistics, 114
U.S. Department of Labor, 107, 117
U.S. Department of the Treasury, 89
U.S. Treasury, 18
uniform, 66, 116
unions, 5
United, v, 48, 55, 58, 60, 106, 114, 120
United Kingdom, 48
United States, v, 55, 58, 60, 106, 114, 120
universe, 88, 108

V

variables, 107
Vice President, 116
volatility, ix, 55
vote, 51

W

wages, 4, 5
Washington, 52, 53, 114, 116, 117, 118, 120, 121
web, 52, 116
White House, 21
White Paper, 119
Wisconsin, 19, 53

withdrawal, viii, 2, 8, 9, 10, 16, 19, 96
workers, viii, 2, 4, 5, 21, 23, 25, 28, 38, 60
workforce, 114
workplace, 32, 36

Y

yield, 49